DEVON AND CORNWALL RECORD SOCIETY

New Series, Vol. 27

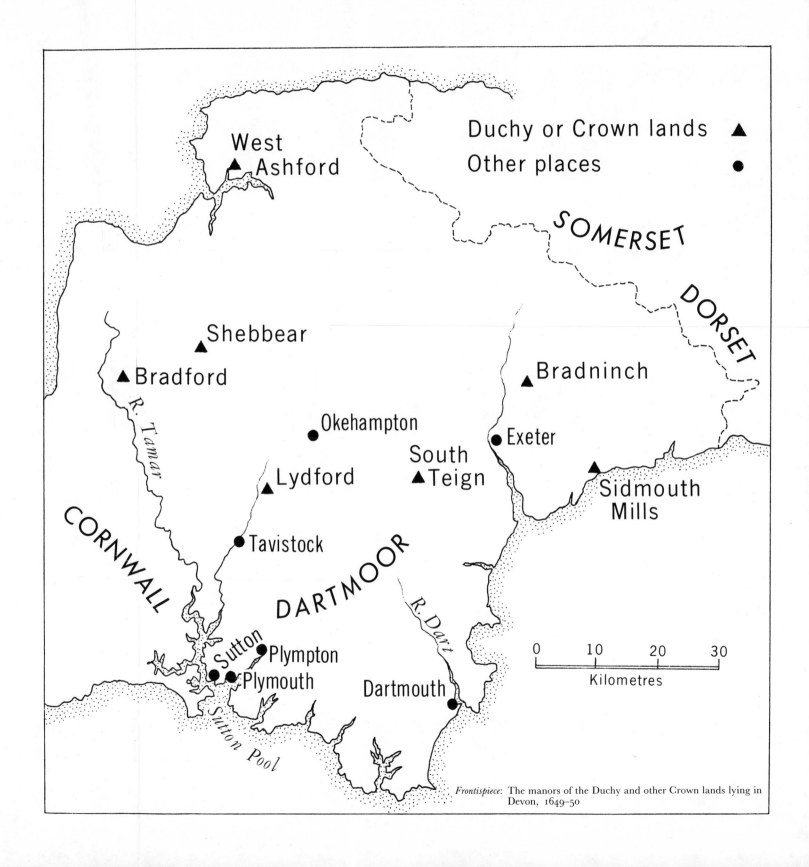

West Ashford

SOMERSET

DORSET

Shebbear

Bradford

Bradninch

R. Tamar

Okehampton

Exeter

South Teign

Lydford

Sidmouth Mills

CORNWALL

Tavistock

DARTMOOR

R. Dart

Sutton

Plympton

Plymouth

Dartmouth

Sutton Pool

Duchy or Crown lands ▲

Other places ●

0   10   20   30

Kilometres

Frontispiece: The manors of the Duchy and other Crown lands lying in Devon, 1649–50

DEVON & CORNWALL RECORD SOCIETY

New Series, Vol. 27

THE PARLIAMENTARY SURVEY OF THE DUCHY OF CORNWALL

PART II
(Isles of Scilly—West Antony and Manors in Devon)

Edited with an Introduction by

NORMAN J. G. POUNDS

Printed for the Society by
THE DEVONSHIRE PRESS LTD.
TORQUAY
ENGLAND

1984

A900

S21

CONTENTS

CORRECTIONS TO PART I

Page 39 line 34 *For* ?Tregay *read* the stream near Tregray

Page 57 lines 41–2 *Read* Nicholas Hender, gt, in his own right, ten. in Trefrew [in Lanteglos], rent 10s, fine 15s.

Page 80 line 7 'Bedam Mill': this phrase, or something very similar, used many times in the survey, clearly derives from *beda molendini* or mill leat.

Page 86 line 3 *For* in St Cleer *read* in Liskeard

Page 87 line 16 *For* Treworgey? *read* Treworgey in Liskeard

line 33 *For* St Pinnock *read* Liskeard

Page 94 line 5 *For* Truro Vean *read* Treworgan in St Erme

Page 95 line 24 *For* Calenick *read* Calerick

Page 96 line 24 *For* Trennick *read* Tresithick in St Erme

Page 105 line 32 *For* in St Anthony in Meneage *read* in Manaccan

Page 114 line 33 *For* Penhale in St Enoder *read* Pollawyn in Colan

line 44 *For* Colan *read* St Columb Minor

lines 47 & 48 *For* St Columb Major *read* St Enoder

Page 115 line 6 *For* St Mawgan *read* St Columb Minor

line 7 *For* ?Rosecliston in Crantock *read* Keskeys in St Columb Minor

line 9 *For* ?Menewink in Lanivet *read* Manuels in St Columb Minor

line 41 *For* in Crantock *read* in St Eval

line 44 *For* Newlyn East *read* Lanhydrock

Page 116 line 46 *For* Colan *read* St Columb Minor

Page 122 line 35 *For* Black Combe? *read* North or South Combe

Page 124 line 3 *For* Berriow in North Hill? *read* Bearah in North Hill

Page 125 line 31 *For* ? *read* id.

line 34 *For* ? *read* Rosecraddoc in St Cleer

INTRODUCTION

The first part of the *Parliamentary Survey of the Duchy of Cornwall* covered the Cornish manors from Austell Prior to Saltash. The second continues from the Isles of Scilly to West Antony, and includes also the manors and other rights that were surveyed in Devon. All formed part of the Duchy of Cornwall, with the exception of the small Devon manors of Shebbear and West Ashford and of Sidmouth Mills. These had on various pretexts escheated to the Crown, and at the time of the survey were Crown property.

The dates when the surveys were made of the Cornish manors are discussed in the Introduction to Part I of the Survey. They were completed, except for the Isles of Scilly, by September 10 1650. The surveys of the Devon manors, with the exception of Bradford and the Borough of Lydford, were made later in the autumn of 1650. An additional survey (no. 64) was made of West Ashford for reasons specified in the survey itself.

The Isles of Scilly were not surveyed until late in the summer of 1652 because of the continued resistance by royalist forces. The survey was made by different surveyors from those who worked on the other manors. The style of their report is fuller and it contains a great deal more information of social and economic significance than the earlier surveys.

For the location of the Cornish manors the reader is referred to the maps in Part I of the Survey. A map of the Devon manors is printed as a frontispiece to this volume.

The editor renews his thanks to those, named in the Introduction to Part I, who have generously given him the benefit of their knowledge. In addition, he wishes to express his gratitude to Professor Charles Thomas and Mr Oliver Padel of the Institute of Cornish Studies for help in identifying place-names. A list of corrections which has been made to Part I appears on page vi. H. R. H. Prince Charles, Duke of Cornwall and his Council have made a further generous contribution towards the cost of publishing Part II.

Department of History,   N. J. G. Pounds
Indiana University

THE PARLIAMENTARY SURVEY OF THE DUCHY OF CORNWALL

37   ISLES OF SCILLY

PRO E 317 (C)/39. There is no copy of this survey in the Duchy Office. The Scillies were surveyed later than other Duchy possessions in Devon and Cornwall, because the Royalist forces continued to hold out here until 1651. The Duchy acquired its lordship over the Isles of Scilly in 1540. They had previously been held by Henry Courtenay, Marquis of Exeter.

'A Survey of all those Islands commonly called the Syllyes alias the Sullyes with the rights, members and appurtences thereof scituate lyeing and being in the Westerne seas within the Countie of Cornewall late parcell of the possessions of Charles Stuart late King of England made and taken by us whose names are hereunto subscribed by vertue of a Commission granted to us by the Hon[ora]ble the Trustees appointed by Act of the Commons assembled in Parliament for sale of the Honnors Mannors and lands heretofore belonging to the late King Queene and Prince under theire hands and seales.

AGNES ILAND

All that Iland . . . commonly called . . . by the name of Agnes Iland [St Agnes] beeing one of the ilands of the Syllyes scituate and withe the parish of St Maries in the Syllies and towards the south of the residue of the islands and neare unto Maries Iland, devided from it by Maryes Sound [St Mary's Sound] as it is nowe devided and parcelled into severall tenements as hereafter followeth:

All that tenement . . . commonly called Needies tenement consisting of a dwelling house and hovell[1] with garden and little close on the backside the said house together with nyne closes or severalls of arable and pasture ground lyeing and beeing for the most part together and all of them neare unto the said dwelling house, conteining all together by estimation nyne acres more or less, now in the tenure and occupacion of John Needye, all which said tenement with appurtenances wee vallue to be worth' p.a. £7.[2]

Hicks ten. consisting of a dwelling house with garden, a 'close called the Common lyeing betwixt this and Needies house and three parcells of arable ground lyeing in a field neare the house of John Traniers, with two parcells of arable lyeing in a field called Isacks Feild, and also two half acres in a feild called Fallow Feild' together 4 ac. now occupied by Henrie Hicks. Value £4 7s.

[1] A hovel was a garden shed or hut, probably used for keeping tools or animals.
[2] The value is given in Roman numerals in a column in the right-hand margin of the page, and the area in Arabic in a column to the left of it.

Nicholas ten., near Tranier's ten., consisting of dwelling house and hovel with garden adjoining and 5 closes of arable and pasture lying intermixed with Needie's closes, by estimation 2¼ ac., now occupied by Peter Nicholas. Valued at £3.

Stevens ten. consisting of dwelling house and hovel with a garden adjoining and 2 parcels of arable in a field near the house and 'one stitch of ground lyeing neare Maries Saound', 2 parcels of arable adjoining the ten. hereafter mentioned in the tenure of Abraham Stevens, in all 6 ac. Value at £5 10s.

Abraham Stevens' ten., consisting of a dwelling house, barn and 2 gardens with a park[3] and close called the Pease Close adjoining the house, with 3 pieces of arable intermixed with Needie's and Nicholas' grounds; also a close called the Gwannaberg; 10 closes 'lyeing together on the South Pease Feild and against St Awanie Sound and a pasture close adjacent to Wing-letang Bay [*id.*] in the said Iland', in all about 12 ac., now occupied by Abraham Stevens. Valued at £10 10s.

Eadie's ten., near the last named, consisting of dwelling house, hovel and garden with 3 closes of arable and pasture adjoining, and 3 closes of arable and pasture lying to the south of Awanies Sound and adjoining Abe Stevens' ten., 4 ac., now occupied by Josias Eadie. Valued at £4.

Richard Hick's ten. near Eadie's, consisting of dwelling house, garden, yard, 2 closes of arable and pasture adjoining J. Eadie's ten; 3 stitches in the field called Churchwaie Field; 2 closes called Chicks Peece lying against St Maries Sound; a little close by the house called Wardfeild, in all 5 ac., occupied by Richard Hicks. Valued at £5.

Bernard Hicks' ten. called Portegles, near Egles Port, consisting of dwelling house, cottage, barn, garden, 5 closes and parcels of arable and pasture adjoining Smiths Sound [Smith Sound] 'and lyeing on the south his dwelling house five closes adjoining the last five closes' and called the Sheep House Close, the Ward Close, the Garden Close, the Cliff Close and the Fore Close, in all 12 ac., occupied by Bernard Hicks. Valued at £13 10s. Md. 'that the garden above said hath been and is the burieing place of the Iland and part of the dwelling was anciently a chappell for the said Iland.'

Traneir's ten. consisting of dwelling house, hovel and backside, the parcel in the field near the said dwelling house 'with an Iland lyeing against Maries Sound devided and severed into six closes or severalls' and 2 closes of arable and pasture 'lyeing neare Portconger in the said Iland', in all 7 ac. Valued at £5 6s 8d.

Michell's ten., near Traneir's, consisting of dwelling house, 2 hovels with gardens thereunto adjoining, with 3 closes of arable and pasture adjoining the house; 3 other closes of arable and pasture 'near Portconger', in all 4 ac. Valued at £2 13s 4d.

Arable and pasture called Callamaye alias May Feild, near the 'last recited parcell'. Occupied by heirs of Richard Hicks dec., ½ ac. Valued at 10s.

---

[3] This appears to be the reading of this contracted term: p'ck.

'There is a storehouse called a Fishhouse formerly used to store the fish in scituate near Portconger afforesaid which is used as a Chappell in the said Iland; also a little barne called a tyth-barne lyeing neare Peter Nicholas house afforemencioned, nowe in the tenure of Mr Pinnock and sometime used to put the tyth corne of the said Island in; both of them beeing used for the publick sevice of the Iland and of soe small vallue therefore we comprehend them in the value of the said Iland for which they are soe used.

There are severall parcells of the said Iland which nowe lye common and are used as commons by the inhabitants of the said Iland' vizt a parcel called Agnes Gue which is 'common lyeing at the east end of the said Ile', two parcels called Wingtertang [Wingletang] Common and Portconger Common lyeing south the last; a parcel called 'the Gowne Common lyeing' on the south side the Iland with other small parcells of the said Iland lyeing in common, all which said commons are for the most part poore barren heathye ground, the sword thereof cut up for furse by the inhabitants of the said Iland, the residue of the said common being used in common for depastureing the cattle belonging to the said inhabitants by reason whereof wee have included the vallue of the said commons in the valluacion of the severall tenements above'. Area by estimate 135 ac.

'And all waies, passages, liberties . . . to the said severall tenements . . . belonging or in any wise apperteining or which have been heretofore used, occupied or enioyed as part, parcell and member of them or any of them.

AGNET [ANNET] ILE
All that Iland with the appurtenances commonly called the Agnett Ile alias Annett Ile . . . scituate . . . to the westward of Agnes Iland . . . devided from Agnes Iland by part of the sea called the Smiths [Smith] Sound and is inviorned by the sea beeing a rockie rugged peece of pasture ground not inhabited, which said Iland is full of cunnie burrogs whereon are but small store of cunnies,[4] haveing been distroyed by the soldiers and others, and in which said cunnie burroghs are the greatest part of the fowle bred which are called the puffins, whereof there are good store in the said Iland, all which said Iland doth conteine by estimacion [40 ac.] . . . which maye bee best improved by a good stock of connies and some goates and maye bee worth' p.a. £4.

'SAMPSONS ILE [SAMSON]
All that Iland . . . called the Sampsons Iland . . . scituate towards the north the Annett Ile . . . and on the north the Broad Sound which parts this and the last Ile and towards the Briars Iland [Bryher] hereafter mencioned and is inviorned with the sea and hath divers rockes called ilands on the east and west thereof, which said ilands called the Sampsons hath been formerlie inhabited by one or two tennants and divers parcells of the same inclosed and improved as arable ground, but the houses and inclosures are now fallen downe and ruined since the takeing of the Syllies from the enemie so that the whole Iland of Sampsons doth now lye wast and is a mountainos rockie ruggie peece of pasture and arable ground now used onelie for some goates and cunnies, all which Iland of Sampson doth

---

[4] i.e. rabbits.

conteine by estimacion [100 ac.] which if it were inhabited and improved might bee worth upon improvement' p.a. £7 10s.

'There are certeine rocks lyeing to the west the Sampsons Iland called by the names of Nornouer[5] Iland or Rock, White [*id.*] Iland or Rock and Castle Bowyer [Castle Bryher] Ile or Rock, and also to the eastward of the Sampson Iland are certeine rocks called the Puffin [*id.*] Iland or Rock, the Greene Iland or Rock [Green Island], the Stone [Stony] Iland or Rock, and the West [Nutt] Island or Rock, all which are for the most part onelie rocks haveing verrie litle or noe grass upon them soe that wee know not how to putt any vallue upon them.

BRYARS ILE [BRYHER]

All that Iland . . . commonly called the Briars Iland . . . scituate . . . in the most westerly of any of the inhabited ilands and towards the northwest of Sampsons Iles . . . being invironed with the sea, haveing on the west the maine Ocean and on the east New Grimsbie Sound [New Grimsby Harbour] and the iland called Tresco [*id.*] . . . all which said iland wee fynd devided into severall tenements and commons vizt'.

Davis ten., commonly called Bartom, lies 'near unto New Grimsbye Sound', with a garden and 4 closes of arable adjoining the house, and 5 closes and parcels of arable and pasture 'lyeing on the south part of William Davis tenement and near the Bancks of the New Poole' and also a close of pasture, in all 9 ac., occupied by James Davis. Valued at £5 10s.

William Davis ten., called the Banton, lying near the Hangmans Ile [Hangman Island] in New Grimsbyes Sound, consisting of dwelling house with garden plot; a parcel of arable called the Backside Close; a close near New Grimsbye Sound; 10 closes of arable and pasture 'under Watchhill [Watch Hill] and adioyninge to James Davises ground'; 5 closes of arable and pasture lying together on the east side of a hill called Gwithiall [Gweal] Hill, in all 15 ac., occupied by William Davis. Valued at £10 10s.

Hoopers ten., called the Bantom and lying near Davis's ten., consisting of dwelling house, garden, plot of ground called Backside Close, 'enioyed together with Davis afforesaid'; a piece of arable in Sheephouse Close; a close called Broad Close, in all 3 ac., occupied by Emanuell Hooper. Valued at £2.

Trevellicks ten., near New Grimbsbyes Sound and under Watchill, consisting of dwelling house, garden, and 2 closes of arable and pasture adjoining, occupied by Margrett Trevelleck, 2½ ac. Valued at £2.

Wallises ten., 'a faire dwelling house with a barne, two gardens and yards thereunto adioyneing', 7 closes and parcels of arable and pasture adjoining the house; a close of arable near Grimsbye, and 5 closes of arable and pasture lying together, 17 ac., lately occupied by 'one Mr Wallis'. Valued at £12 10s.

'GWITHIALL ILE [GWEAL ISLAND]

There is a litle iland called Gwithiall Iland lyeing to the north-west the

[5] The map suggests that Mincarlo was intended.

Briars Iland and is therewith used and occupied as a common thereunto belonging, conteining eight acres more or less.

There are also divers parcells of Bryars Iland which are used occupied and enioyed by all the inhabitants of Briars Iland as commons belonging to theire tenements vizt one parcell being the north part of the said Iland called Sheepenhead [Shipman Head], one parcell west Sheepenhead called Gwithiall Hills [Gweal Hill]; one parcell called the Watch Hill; one parcell lyeing neare the Fresh Poole, and one parcell called the Heathy Hill lyeing toward the south end of this iland, with other small parcells, all which said commons and parcells doe conteine [280 ac.] but are for the most part barren heathy ground and used in common by the inhabitants of the said iland for serving and depastureing of theire catle belonging to theire severall tenements, all which wee vallue to be worth' p.a. £10.

'And all waies, passages, liberties . . . to the said severall tenements belong . . . or which have been heretofore used, occupied or enioyed as part, parcell and member of them or any of them.

There are certaine rocks lyeing to the westward of Briars Iland called by the names of Mevawllin Iland or Rock and Syllyes Iland or Rock [Scilly Rock], and also one rock to the eastward called Hangmans Iland [Hangman Island] or Rock, all which said ilands or rocks are onely rocks that have noe soyle left to beare grass thereon.

There is a Sound called Newgrimflow [New Grimsby Harbour] Sound on the east Briars Iland passing between Brar [Bryher] and Tresco Iland wherein a great number of ships maye ride of any burthen.

TRESKOE ILAND [TRESCO]

All that Iland . . . called Treskoe Iland scituate . . . towards the east of Briars Ile afforesaid haveing on the north the maine Ocean, on the east Old Grimsbye and on the south part of the Crow Sound [*id.*], all which said Iland of Treskoe wee find devided and severed into severall tenements and commons as hereafter followeth vizt:

All that tenement . . . called the Abbye tenement scituate towards the south west part of the said Iland at a place called the Abbey [Tresco Abbey], consisting of a dwelling house and three closes or parcells of arable and pasture ground called the North Close lyeing neare the said house, all which said tenement and appurtenances are now in the tenure and occupacion of Michall Chester doe conteine by estimacon [3 ac.] . . . which wee vallue' at £2.

Sincocks ten. 'sometimes parcell of the said Abbey scituate neare unto the tenement last recited', consisting of dwelling house, garden plot and divers parcel of arable and pasture, viz. half of the closes called South Close adjoyning the house, Yate Close lying near the house, the Apletree Close near Newgrimsbye Sound, 2 closes called Longbrakes, near Poole [Great Pool], and Edgers Ground hereafter mentioned, in all 7 ac., occupied by John Sincock. Worth £5.

Jenkins ten., once part of the Abbey and situated near the last, consisting of dwelling house with divers parcels of arable and pasture, viz. half of the Southfeild aforementioned, and a little close adjoining the Abbey; also a close called Brake Close lying near the Poole and a close called the Plomp Close near the last named, in all 5 ac., occupied by John Jenkins. Valued at £3 10s.

Abbey ten., part of the said Abbey and lying near the last, consisting of a dwelling house and several parcels of arable and pasture, namely 'half of that close before the gate before mentioned called the Gate Close'; also the Apletree Close adjoining Grimsby Sound and a close called the Longbrake, in all 3 ac., occupied by William Odger. Valued at £2.

Dennis ten. consisting of dwelling house, garden and divers parcels of arable and pasture, namely 3 little closes 'lyeing neare the Leager against New Grimsbye Sound'; 2 brake closes near the New Pooles, in all 2 ac., occupied by David Dennis. Valued at £1 10s.

Trevaricks ten. on the south side of Windmill Hill, consisting of dwelling house and 2 parcels of arable and pasture called the Home Ground lying near the dwelling house, with 2 other parcels, in all 3 ac., occupied by David Treverick. Valued at £2 6s 8d.

Cottage near Trevericks House, now in the tenure of Joseph Ansell. Valued at 10s.

Ansells ten., consisting of dwelling house and park near New Grimsbye, with a close of arable and pasture under Windmill Hill and another close on the east of Windmill Hill, in all 4 ac., occupied by John Ansell. Valued at £3.

Bickfords ten., consisting of dwelling house and park, with 2 closes of arable and pasture, near the east end of New Poole, in all 1½ ac., occupied by relict of Henry Bickford. Valued at £1 10s.

Jenkinses ten., near Bickfords ten., consisting of dwelling house and home ground and 2 closes of arable and pasture, in all 2 ac., occupied by Stephen Jenkins. Valued at £1 13s 4d.

Watts Close, a ruined ten., and close of arable and pasture between the closes of Withers and Downeing, of 3 roods, in tenure of William Watts. Valued at 12s.

Prides ten., consisting of dwelling house near Dover Fort in Iland with a close of arable and pasture near the house, 1¼ ac., occupied by Katherine Pride. Valued at £1 6s 8d.

Hoopers ten., consisting of garden and arable close near Dover Fort, 1¼ ac., occupied by John Hooper. Valued at £1 6s 8d.

Treverick ten. consisting of dwelling house, garden, an arable close near Dover Fort and another arable close nearby, 1¼ ac., occupied by Emanuell Trenerrick. Valued at £1 10s.

Withers Cottage with garden 'against the Sandy Bay neare Dover Fort', occupied by William Withers. Valued at 10s.

Storehous ten., against Old Grimsbye Sound, consisting of 5 houses with yards and gardens, several closes and parcels of arable and pasture, namely Storehouse Close, Fishhous Close (both adjoining the dwelling house),

Well Close, Barne Close, 'with a barne standing therein', New Grimsby Close, Blackberrie Close, and 3 closes and parcels near New Grimsby, in all 32½ ac., occupied by Walter Hooper. Valued at £1 10s.

Rabmants ten., consisting of dwelling house and 4 closes and parcels of arable and pasture, in all 2 ac., occupied by John Rabmant. Valued at £1 10s.

Cornish cottage and garden, occupied by Henrie Cornish. Worth 6s 8d.

Parcells in the Lord's possession; parcells of arable and pasture occupied by the Farmer of the island, namely 4 closes on the east of Jenkins', lately Ansties and Stoles; a close to the east of Bickfords; 2 closes lately Vance lying against Crow Sound near New Poole; 2 closes lately Ansells, lying east of the last; a close lately Withers adjacent to the last 4 closes lately Downeings, and Waters lying north-east of the last; a storehouse or fish-house near Mr Hooper's house 'used for the storeing of the ling and conger', in all 12 ac. Valued at £5 16s 8d.

'There are parcells of the said Iland which are commons and are now used . . . as common by the inhabitants and tennants of the said Iland vizt the common called Crow More lyeing toward the southwest of the said Iland towards the Crow Sound, also a common called the Abbie Hill lyeing on the north side the Abbey, also a common called the Windmill Hill Common lyeing towards the east neare to Grimsbie whereon Dover Fort is built, also a common called the Castle Downe Common lyeing neare to New Grims-bye Sound and whereon stands the walls of an old Fort or Castle and on which common upon a rock there is a new blockhouse [now Cromwell's Castle] building to command the New Grimsbye Sound, all which said commons are poore barren heathy and hilly ground, used by the severall tenants of the said Iland for fireing and depastureing of theire catle', 400 ac. Valued at £15.

'There is a Sound called Old Grimsbye Sound upon the north east this Iland from the North Sea passing betweene this Iland and Norworthell [Northwethel] and is a reasonable good sound for ships to ride in towards Dover Fortt.

NORWOTHILL [NORTHWETHEL] ILAND
All that Iland . . . commonly called Norwothill Iland alias Arwothill scitu-ate . . . towards the north east of the Iland Tresco . . . and on the north to Dover Fort . . . and is on the north east of Old Grimsbie Sound which said Iland hath noe other improvement made thereof but onely for connies and might depasture some goates and contenieth' by estimation 15 ac. Valued at 7s 6d.

'HELLINS ILAND [ST HELENS ISLAND]
. . . the St Hellins Iland scituate . . . towards the north east of the Iland Arwothell . . . and towards the North Sea, which said Iland is a rockie hill wherein are some store of conny berries, not many coninges thereon have-ing been destroyed of late by the soulderie but is a rough heathy peece of ground which may bee best improved by depasturing sheep or goates and connies', 35 ac. Worth [blank]

'Round Iland [Round Island]

There is a little iland commonly called the Round Iland scituate . . . towards the north east of the Hellens Ile . . . and is a rocky pore peece of ground wherein are some connie berries and connies, but is of verrie litle or noe vallue by reason of the beating or dashing of the sea by reason whereof noe other catle cann be able to live there.

Tean Iland [Tean Island]

All that . . . Tean Iland scituate . . . towards the south east of Hellins Ile and on the west Tean Sound and St Martins Iland, in which said Iland there did dwell one inhabitant before the takeing of the Iland from the enimie, whose house is now ruined, which said iland hath in it store of Connie berries and connies, but is a rockie drye hillie peece of ground which may best be improved by depastureing of sheepe, goates and connies', area 35 ac.

'There is a Sound upon the east this Iland from the North Sea passing betwixt this and Martins Iland, which Sound was but lately discovered and is not so good as eyther of the Grimsbye Sounds'.

Md. 'that the Sampson Iland, Tresco Iland, Arwothell, St Hellins the Round Il. and and the Teane Iland as wee are informed are claimed by Sir William Godolphin, but by what right wee knowe not neither was any such claime to the said Ilands tendred unto us.

St Martins Iland [St Martins]

. . . scituate towards the north east of all the Scyllye Ilands and on the east of the Teane Sound, haveing on the north thereof Whites Iland [White Island] and the North Sea, in which said Iland are onely two poore inhabitants, those formerlie that did dwell there beeing ruined by the enimees souldeirye so that most part of there tenements nowe laye wast or common with the residue of the said Iland wherein are onely two tenements vizt.

Jenkins ten., near Teane Sound at the west end of the island, consisting of dwelling house and 4 little parcels of arable near the house, 1 ac., occupied by Gregorie Jenkins. Valued at £1.

Shakerleys ten., near Jenkin's ten., consisting of dwelling house barn and 2 parcels of arable near the house, 1 ac., occupied by Francis Shakerley. Valued at £1.

'All the residue of the said Iland lyeth common, part whereof hath been arable ground of the quantitie of about [100 ac.]. The residue of the said Iland is a hillie brakey and rockey peece of ground wherein are many cunnie berries and connyes, and may bee best improved for the most part thereof by depastureing of sheep, goates or any other catle, beeing a larg peece of ground conteining in all [by estimation 1000 ac. Worth £2 10s].

Whites Iland [White Island]

There is a litle round iland commonly called Whites Iland scituate . . . on the north west part of the said Iland St Martins and adioining thereto by the

Beech or Sand and is used . . . with the Iland St Martins wherein are some connies, which said iland conteine [12 ac. and is worth 6s.]

KNOLLMORE ILE [NORNOUR ISLAND]
There is a rock or litle iland lyeing toward the south the head of St Martins called Knollmore Iland which is of litle or noe vallue by reason of the dashing of the sea.

GOONEHYLLYE ILANDS [GREAT AND LITTLE GANILLY]
. . . the Gret Goonehillye and the Litle Goonehyllye beeing two hills or rocks in one iland scituate . . . on the south the head of St Martins Iland, which said iland is a rockey rough ground wherein are bred store of sea fowle and some connies and may be best improved by connyes or goates, and conteineth . . .', 40 ac. and is worth £1.

'There are certaine rocks commonly called the Menenwethell Ile [Menawethan], the Enis Fold Ile [Great and Little Innisvouls] and the Ragged Iland [Ragged Island] scituate . . . on the east and south the Goonehyllyes which are onely rocks and of no vallue nor capeable of improvement.

ARTHURS ILAND [GREAT AND LITTLE ARTHUR ISLANDS]
. . . scituate . . . on the south the Goonehyllyes and the Litle Ilands . . . lyeing against the Crow Sound on the south, which said iland is three rockye hills wherein are some connyes and sea fowle bred but is a rockey rough brakey peece of ground and may bee best improved by connyes and goates . . .', 30 ac. Worth 15s.

'There are certaine rocks commonly called Litle Kenenick Iland [Little Ganinick], the Great Kenenicks Iland [Grat Ganinick], the Brighall [Biggal] Rocks and other rocks which lye on the east, south and west the Arthurs Iland, which are onely rocks and of noe vallue.

There is a Sound upon the south and south west all these ilands of St Martins and the rest last recyted which is commonly called the Crow Sound passing betweene these and St Maries Iland through which sound is a derect passage from the maine land unto St Maries and to the Castle and Hue [Hugh Town, St Mary's] therein, which is a reasonable good sound for ships to ryde in neare the Hue.

ST MARIES ILAND [ST MARY'S]
. . . beeing the cheife iland of the Scyllyes scituate towards the south and south east of all the said ilands beeing inviorned with the sea, haveing on the south thereof the maine ocean, on the south west the Maries Sound, on the west the Broade Sound and on the west and north the Crow Sound, beeing devided and severed into severall parts and tenements as hereafter followeth, leaving the Hue Hill, the Castle, the Storehouses and the demesnes unto the latter end of the survey of the said iland'.

Cott. with garden, 'neare a place called Carnye Thomas', occupied by Anthonye Curney. Worth 10s.

Ten. occupied by Peter Phillips, consisting of dwelling house, garden and 2 closes of meadow and arable, 2½ ac. Worth £2 10s.

Cott. occupied by one Kewbert [margl. note Cubert], with a garden, on the south side of Carney Thomas.

Ten. called Carthue, near cottage last mentioned and 'unto the hill called Bussies Hill [Buzza Hill], now occupied by Lewis Callamaie, consisting of dwelling house with park and garden, a close and parcel of arable adjoining Busses Hill, and 6 other closes of arable and pasture in Carthue adjacent to Widdowe Shackerleys ten., 9 ac. Worth 6s.

Ten. called Carthue adjoining Busses Hill, consisting of dwelling house and 5 closes of arable and pasture, now occupied by Arner Shakerley wid., 4 ac. Worth 3s.

Ten. occupied by Salloman Gwenip, consisting of dwelling house and garden adjacent to Harris' ten., with closes of arable and pasture, namely a close near Portcreso; a close part of Gwernegavells ten.; a park adjoining 'to the cottage used for diseased people', and another close of Gwevernegavells ten. adjacent to the 'litle centrie hereafter mencioned', 2 ac. Worth £2 15s.

Cott. occupied by Stephen Bennett with garden 'on the west side of Busses Hill and neare unto Port Creso [Porth Cressa].'

Cott. occupied by John Summers with garden near Wid. Shakerley's ground. Worth £1.

Cott. occupied by George Phillips with garden in Carthie and on the south side of Bussies Hill, adjoining Wid. Shakerleys ground. Worth 13s 4d.

Ten. called Churchtowne Bargaine, occupied by Ann Christopher wid., consisting of dwelling house and garden near St Maryes Church, with 6 closes of arable and pasture 'lyeing together neare the said Church' and also 2 closes called the Tregarden Waltha adjoining Chinnans grounds, 10 ac. Worth £7.

Cott. and garden occupied by Nicholas Cheanhall, worth £1.

2 cotts and 4 gardens occupied by Alexander Duff or his assigns adjoining the Churchyard. Worth £2.

Close of arable called Litle Centrie, occupied by Richard Somers, 1¼ ac. Worth £1 10s.

Ten. occupied by John Harris, consisting of dwelling house and garden adjoining Phillipes, with 2 closes, part of Gwernegavell ten. and adjoining the Great Centrie, and also a close and 2 parks adjoining the Litle Centrie, 3 ac. Worth £4.

Cott. and garden adjoining Harris's ten., occupied by Clement Rowe. Worth 10s.

Cott. and garden, as above, occupied by John Phillips. Worth 6s 6d.

THE OLD TOWN NEAR THE OLD CASTLE [ENNOR CASTLE]

Cott. and garden 'neare the Old Castle in the Old Towne', occupied by Henrie Gwinep [margl. Gwenip], worth 10s; Cott. and garden adjoining the above, occupied by John Gwinop, 10s;   Cott. and garden, as above, occupied by Marie Bozow, 10s;   Cott. 'neare the Old Castle' with a garden in Tollmans Field, occupied by Nicholas Thomas, 15s;   Cott. and garden in the Old Town, occupied by Tristrum John, 6s 8d;   Cott. and garden adjoining the last, occupied by William Carvagh, 6s 8d;   Cott. and garden situated against the last, occupied by Phillip Reynolds, 6s 8d;   Cott. and garden, as above, occupied by Discipline Rogers, 6s 8d;   Cott., hovel and half a garden near the last, occupied by Robert Callamaye, 10s;   Cott. and half a garden, as above, occupied by Joseph Calamaye, 6s 8d;   Cott. near the last, occupied by William Hellin, 2s 6d;   Cott. and garden, as above, occupied by Margret Searle, 10s;   Cott. and garden occupied by Sible Renfrye, 10s;   Cott. adjoining the last 'with a garden in Castle Close', occupied by Richard Lucas, 10s;   Ten. and garden adjoining the last, occupied by Mr Robert Flamock, 26s 8d;   Cott. and shop, as above, occupied by Richard Somers, 15s;   Cott. and smith's shop, as above, occupied by Edward Nicholas, 2s;   Cott. and garden, as above, occupied by Thomas Drake, 10s.

Ten. consisting of dwelling house and garden in the Old Town and adjoining Drake's, with divers closes and parcels of arable and pasture, namely a close part of Kearngwavell, adjoining Gwinop's; 2 close adjoining the latter; a park adjoining Gwinop's cott.; a little common adjoining the said park, in all 3 ac. £3 10s.

Cott. and garden adjoining Rosver's dwelling house, occupied by John Stoddin [marg. Stoden], 10s; Cott. and garden adjoining the last, occupied by Henrie Greebye, 6s 8d;   Cott. adjoining the last, now a stable called the Dyehouse alias Reyhouse, occupied by the Governor of the Island, 6s 8d;   2 cotts and a hovel with 2 gardens, near the last, occupied by Ann Pepwell, £1 5s; Cott. and garden behind the last, occupied by Richard Ford, 15s;   Cott. and garden adjoining the last, occupied by Bampford Bernard, 12s;   Cott. and garden near the last, occupied by Nicholas Reynolds, 6s 8d   Cott. and garden, as above, occupied by Thomas Trevillian, 10s;   Cott. and garden, occupied by Augustine Urian, 10s; Cott. and garden near the last, occupied by John Renfrye, 15s;   Cott. and garden, occup. John Capell, 15s;   Cott. and garden adjoining the last, occup. Samuell Trevennick [marg. Trevinick], 12s;   Cott. and garden near the last, occup. Edward Nicholas, 12s;   Cott. and garden near the last, occup. Francis Christopher, 15s;   Cott. and garden adjoining the last, occup. Georg [sic] Webber 15s.

Ten. consisting of dwelling house and garden in the Old Towne near the last, with 4 closes of arable and pasture at Carney Thomas, in all 4 ac., occup. Edward Searle, £3 15s.

2 cotts and gardens adjoining Searle's house, occup. Thomas Morecock, 15s;   Ten. and garden near the last, occup. John Pinnock, £1 10s;   Ten. and garden near the Old Castle, with a close of arable and pasture called Great Centrie lying near Duffe's ten., 4 ac., occup. Thomas Barnes, 6s 10d;   Cott. and garden in Newfort, occup. Francis Restorick, 10s;   Cott. and garden adjoining Restorick's cott., occup. Elizabeth Phillips wid., 6s 8d;   Ten. and garden in Newford, occup. Michell Toll,

6s 8d;   3 cotts. with gardens and close adjoining on the east side of the Newfort Hill, occup. Georg Phillips, 1 ac., £1 10s; Cott., garden and adjoining park near the last, occup. Ciprian Thomas, £1;   Ten. consisting of house, 6 closes of arable and pasture, 4 closes of 'downes', all at Helvere near Francis, 36 ac., occup. Widdow Watts, £9.

Ten. consisting of 3 cotts. with gardens and 4 closes of arable and pasture 'scituate over the Moore', 5 ac., occup. Widdow Watts, £6.

2 ten. called 'Chinnans tenements or farme', consisting of 2 dwelling houses with gardens, 5 closes of arable and pasture, 2 closes of arable called the Great Closes, 3 closes called [Parting Carn] lying near the More, 2 closes called the New Closes 'adioning to the home ground', another ten. and garden adjoining the New Close with a close called the Creek Dew adjacent to the Newcloses. 14 ac., occup. Ellis Jenkins and Francis Watts, £12.

Ten. consisting of 2 dwelling houses and gardens, 4 closes and parcels of arable and pasture called the Creekdew, 3 ac., occup. Thomas Bickford, £2 6s 8d.

Ten. called Tremalthen [marg. Tremelethan], consisting of dwelling house with a barn and gardens near Jenkins and Bickford's, with 13 closes and parcels of meadow, pasture and arable, 18 ac., occup. Marye Callemaye, £15.

High Cross ten, consisting of 'two poore cottages with gardens', 6 closes and parcels of arable and pasture to the north of the house, 2 parks and a close to the south, adjoining the Castle Feild; a close called the Moore in Hallevale [Holy Vale] and a Downe adjoining, in all 26 ac., occup. John Hooper, £9.

Cott. called Drums House, garden and close near Hookers, 1¼ ac., occup. Francis Urian £1 6s 8d.

Sallakeys [Salakee] ten. consisting of 'a faire dwelling house with a barne, mault house, outhouses with gardens and [16] closes of meddow, pasture, arable and morye grounds' adjoining and a down called the Wardhill Downe lying to the south of her other grounds, in all 88 ac., occup. Mrs Prudence Lewis, £22.

Ten. called Midle Normandye [Normandy] consisting of dwelling house with gardens and 7 closes or parcels of arable and pasture, with a cottage and garden called Kernefriars [Carn Friars] a close called the More; half a close with Francis Legg called the Moore in Halivale; a close called the Long Close with a park and close adjoining Kerne Friars; a close near the Moore; a close lying behind Hancock's ten.; 'half of Meane Teddin [Mount Todden] Downe which hee holds with Mr Hancock', in all 36 ac., occup. Lewis Morris, £11.

Ten. called Higher Normandye: dwelling house, barn, outhouses and gardens, with 10 closes of arable and pasture; half a close called the Moore in Hallevale; part of a common 'lyeing to the sea'; part of a common with Morris and Harris, in all 30 ac., occup. Francis Legg, £10 10s.

Cott. and garden 'neare Portlistrye [Toll's] Iland against the Crow Sound'. 4s.

Kernie Friars [Carn Friars] ten.: dwelling house, garden, 2 closes of arable
and pasture called the Home Ground on the north of the dwelling house; a
close called the Moore lying near Harrises Moore; 6 closes adjoining the
Home Ground; moiety of a down called Meane Teddon Downe 'lyeing on
the north [of] Carvagh along by the sea a little past Mean Teddon Fort,
which he holds together with Lewis Morris, and part of a down with Morris
and Carvagh, 45 ac., £9.

Kearnsedg ten.: 2 little dwelling houses with garden and 8 closes of arable
and pasture called Kearnsedg Closes, with a close in Hallivale called the
Moore and 4 closes called Furzie and Heallye Downes adjoining the Moore,
25½ ac., occup. Robert Harris, £8.

Lower Normandie ten.: 2 dwelling houses with garden; 12 closes or parcels
of arable and pasture lying together near Hancock's ten; a close in Hallivale
called the Moore; a large down called the White Street Downe near
Phellecks port [Porth Hellick] and adjoining the ten. and the East Sea; also
moiety of a down with Mr Hancock and Morris, 74 ac., occup. Ursula
Carvagh, £12 10s.

Longstone ten.: dwelling house, barn and garden; 7 closes of arable and
pasture with a down adjoining, all lying near the house; a close called the
Moore in Hallevale, 16 ac., occup. Mrs Saragh Treweek, £13.

Halivale ten.: 'a faire dwelling house with large outhouses and gardens'; 21
closes and parcels of meadow, pasture and arable and morie ground in and
about Hallevale; part of Portlistree [Pelistry] Down and also Portlistree
Iland [Toll's Island], 160 ac., occup. Mr Deggerye Cloake, £30.

Little Toller ten.: dwelling house with outhouses and garden near the last; 8
closes and a park of arable and pasture adjoining the house, 8 ac., occup.
John Skinnar, £6 13s 4d.

Great Toller ten.: dwelling house with outhouses and gardens; 6 closes and
parcels of arable and pasture; 2 closes of pasture; a down lying against the
Crow Sound, 24½ ac., occup. Thomas Bant, £9 10s.

Helvere [Helvear] ten.: 2 dwelling houses with outhouses and gardens; 7
closes of arable and pasture adjoining; 6 closes of arable and pasture in
Hallevere, near Morris's ten. [next mentioned]; a common down near
Halevale, 32 ac., occup. Francis Urian and William Urian, £10 10s.

Helvere ten.: 3 cotts or little dwelling houses with gardens; 7 closes of arable
or pasture adjoining; a common called Hallevere Common, 30 ac., occup.
Jane Morris wid., £10.

Trennowith [Trenoweth] ten.: dwelling house and garden; 6 closes of
arable and pasture adjoining near Widow Water's land; a close adjoining
Helvere Common; 2 closes to the east of and adjoining the last, 17 ac.,
occup. John Tringove, £8.

Helvere Common, adjoining the last, 40 ac., occup. John Tringove and
Francis Urian, £2 5s.

Newfort [Newford] ten.: a 'faire dwelling house with large outhouses gardens, orchards with closes and common adjacent, all lying together under

the New Fort', with 7 close of arable and pasture near John Tringoves, 'with a cottage therein and also 4 closes to the south of the last 7 closes; 2 closes or downs on the south and west of the last and adjoining them; 4 closes called Taylor's closes lying together on the south of [Carn Morval] Rock and against Mr Couch's cliff closes', 160 ac., occup. Lawrence Pim, £24.

Michells ten.: dwelling house and garden to west of Mr Pim's land, with 4 closes and parcels of arable and pasture adjoining; 2 'poore furzie downes' north west of Mr Pim's; 2 commons to south of the Crow, 40 ac., occup. George Michell, £5.

Saras ten.: dwelling house, garden and 2 closes near the last; a close to the west of John Evan's house; moiety of 4 downs near the Barr of Pendrithen, 7 ac., occup. Julian Sara wid., £3.

Evan's ten.: dwelling house and garden; an arable close near 'Barnses last recyted close'; 3 closes of arable and pasture near Widow Sara's land; moiety of 4 downs near the Barr of Pendrethun, 6 ac., occup. [   ], £3 10s.

Purthlaw [Porthloo] ten.: dwelling house with garden and close adjoining, near Evan's house, with 'a large downe' on the south of (—) Michell's Downe; a close at Catt Iland; 3 closes of meadow and arable 'against the Catt Iland on the east Mr Crowches house and one close hereafter mentioned and adjacent thereto'; 3 closes of arable and pasture near Mr Cowches 4 closes; a little meadow at the Mooreside near Wid. Wats' ground, 28 ac., occup. Sampson Vallack, £5.

Purthlaw ten. near the last: 'large dwelling house with gardens' and 4 closes of arable; 2 other arable closes north-east of Mr Vallack's house; a large downe lying against Crow Sound and to the south of Mr Vallack's down; a close called Cliff Close 'against the Catt Iland', 100 ac., occup. Mr Crowch. £12.

Terungoe ten.: dwelling house, barn and garden; 5 closes of arable and pasture adjoining; 4 closes or commons near the house, 15 ac., occup. William Vrian, £6.

Hooper's Cott. and garden at Terungo,; part of a down with Hooper, hereafter mentioned, occup. Alexander Hooper, 13s 4d;   Tomlin's cott. and garden, near the last, occup. John Tomlins, 13s 4d.

Tregarthingrill ten.: dwelling house and gardens; 10 closes or parcels of meadow, arable and pasture lying together and near the house; 2 downs called the Persevells; part of a down with Hooper aforesaid, 26 ac., occup. Henrie George, £7.

Trewins [Trewince] ten.: dwelling house and garden; 10 closes or parcels of arable and pasture near the house; common down near Wats, 12 ac., occup. Jenkin Griffin, £5.

IN THE HUGH OR NEW TOWNE NEAR THE NEW CASTLE

Cope's ten. near 'the brewhouse for the garison in the Hugh or New Towne', occup. John Cope, 8s;   Thomases ten. and garden, near last, occup. James Thomas, 16s;   Lewises ten. near last, occup. Jonathan Lewis, £3;   Provases ten. with hovel, outhouses and garden, near the last, occup. Thomas Provas, £3; Leggs ten. and garden, near last, occup. Haniball Legg, 16s; Mr Hooper's ten.: 2 ten. 'late erected' with garden, occup. Mr Walter Hooper or his assigns, £4.

Griffin's ten.: dwelling house and garden with 2 closes or parcels of arable near Rosvere's ground; a close adjoining Mr Collyer's Peninis [Peninnis] hereafter mentioned, 3½ ac., occup. Mathew Griffin, £9.

Hooper's ten. 'with an oast to drye mault upon . . . thereunto belonging', near last. occup. John Hooper, 16s; Rippses ten., occup. William Ripps, £1 5s; Williams' ten., near last, occup. Thomas Williams, 6s 8d; George Hooper's ten., near last, £6; Hutchin's ten., near last, occup. John Hutchins, 5s; Sanders' ten., occup. John Sanders, 16s; Chinhall's ten. 'with smiths shop and garden', occup. William Chinhall, £3 10s.

Mr Collyer's ten. 'a faire dwelling house being an Inn commonly called The George in the Hugh . . . with a sellar and gardens adjoining and belonging' with 4 closes of meadow, arable and pasture near the lands of Peter Phillips and near Carnye Thomas; also a close called Penenis [Peninnis] adjoining Rosvere's grounds. 4½ ac., occup. Mr John Collyer, £12.

'There are divers parcells of land and some tenements in this Iland the most part whereof hath been counted demesnes and alwaies in the possession of the Governor of the said Iland and as wee are informed they have been possessed and imployed in relation to the Government and Garison and are as followeth:
Brewhouse and Pump Close, arable, in the Hugh, 2½ ac., £9.
Salter's ten. and garden, 'commonly imployed and occupied by the surgeon of the said Garrison', £6.
High Meadow, adjoining Phillipses meadow, 1½ ac., £1 10s.
Rymeddows: 2 closes of 'moorey grounds' called Rymeddows alias Rymoores, adjoining the last, 2½ ac., £2.
2 closes or parcels of meadow and morey ground' called Kearngravell Moores, 3 ac., £2 5s.
Close and parcel of 'morye ground' called the Round Burrogh Moore, adjoining the last, 3 ac., £2.
Close and parcel of meadow or 'measley ground' called Horsemoore, adjoining Rymeddowes on the south, 5 ac., £5.
4 closes of meadow and pasture called the Towne Moores to the north of Rymeddows, 7 ac., £5.
Close called the Long Close adjoining the Old Castle, 2½ ac., £2 5s.
'The Old Castle stands in this close but is a quarter and garison for the preservation of the Church port by the Old Towne and is of little or noe vallue for any other use.'
Close of arable and pasture called the Castle Feild, near the Old Castle, 6 ac., £5.
Close of arable and pasture called the Tolmans Feild, adjoining the last, 5 ac., £3 10s.
3 closes of arable and pasture called the Drums Ground, 6 ac., £4 10s.
Close of meadow called the Tregarden Close, 2 ac., £1 10s.
Kearngowgy Downe, 'almost spoyled with cutting for turf', with the

Broome Close, both adjoining Castle Feild and the south sea, 10 ac., £2 10s.

Close of 'moorye ground' called the Lords Moore in the Hallevale, 3½ ac., £3 10s.

Close of 'moorye ground' called the Lords Moore in Hallevale, adjoining Harrises Moore, 2½ ac., £2 10s.

Down called Kernmarva Downe, against the Crow Sound and south of Mr Crouch's Down, 85 ac., £4.

Fish Seller in the Old Towne, 'consisting of two roomes below staires and two above staires with a counting house neare thereunto, both situate neare unto Renfryes dwelling house', £1 10s.

'There is a new storehouse called the Stone Storehouse scituate in the Hugh . . . and neare Mr Collyers house . . . consisting of two roomes belowe staires and two above staires nowe used as a storehouse for the provisions of the garrison, £4.

Also the new boarded storehouse . . . neare the last, being a verrie large house devided into fowre roomes below staires and one long roome above', now used as a storehouse for the garrison's provisions, £8.

Md. 'Wee are informed that both these storehouses were lately built by the enimye and redemed for money upon the reducing of the said Ilands.'

'Also another storehouse called the Salthouse scituate at the north end of Mr Collyers house . . . consisting of a seller below staires and a loft above. . .', £2.

'Also all that other storehouse called the salt seller scituate near the last', 13s 4d.

'All that storehouse scituate . . . neare the Key consisting of two roomes below staires and three above, with a court and shedd for coles; also another court with a shed and carpenters shop therein, nowe used and imployed for the use of the Garison', £6 13s 4d.

'There is a common called Penenis [Peninnis] Comon and divers other small parcells of wast and common and highwaie ground lyeing dispersed in this Iland and intermixably enioyed by the inhabitants', estimated 300 ac. Its value is included in the tenements.

THE HUGH-HILL

'The residue of the Maryes Iland is called the Hughhill and is that part of the said Iland where in the New Castle now stand and is fortifyed round the said hill with a lyne and severall bulworkes and platformes thereon and is the cheif strenth of all the said Ilands wherein is the Castle and severall litle tenements and storehouses, all of them used and imployed by and for the use of the garison . . . and is as followeth:

The Castle is built in the forme of an acute octogon fort with a good stone rampaire of the same forme, but verrie low and litle consisting of a hall or new roome, butterye and two sellers with a kitchin, pastrye and larder below staires with a dyneing roome and fowre chambers in the second storie and seaven litle roomes over them with fowre litle turrets upon the leads, also upon the rampere and over the port are five litle roomes for the gunners stores and under the rampere and at the port is a court and guard and fowre other litle roomes for stores also.' Worth p.a. £13 6s 8d.

Bakehouse: 'All that storehouse scituate under the Hugh hill betweene the Castle and the sea, consisting of a bakeing house, a bunting house and two other roomes below staires and a dairye and three other roomes above staires together with a brewhouse at the end of it with a slaughter house and a loft over it thereunto adioyneing with other necesarye roomes thereunto adioyneing and belonging, all which are now used and imployed for the service of the garison, which might be worth' p.a. £5.

Coles house: 'All that tenement or dwelling house . . . commonly called Doctor Coles lodgings scituate on the side of the Hugh Hill neare the Castle and the Bakehouses . . . consisting of one roome below staires and two roomes above staires which said house is now a quarter for one of the Captains of the garrison and which might bee worth' p.a. 10s.

Fish House: '. . . neare the Castle Gate now used . . . as a storehouse for the garrison', worth 2s 6d.

Two barns and a stable 'standing upon the side of the said Hugh hills now imployed for the service of the said garison', 10s.

'Two Smithes shops on the side of Hugh Hills and neare unto the Castle nowe imployed in the service of the garison', £1.

Ten. and garden called Wid. Striblins ten. on the side of High Hill, 13s 4d; Little ten. called Bennetts House, with garden, near last, 13s 4d; Little ten. near the Windmills, called Grills House, 6s 8d; Little ten. and garden called Gwinops ten. on Hugh Hill, 6s 8d.

'An old Fort called the Follye which is onely the old walls and shedderd within for the quartering of soldiers, scituate towards the south end of the Hugh Hill', £1.
Another house called the Steeveall on the west of Hugh Hill, now a quarter for the soldiers, 10s.

'Two windmills standing neare the midle of the Hugh Hill on the south the Castle, which are the mills imployed for the service of the garrison of all the Ilanders, with all the soake, toll, suite and custome thereunto belonging', £100.

The Hugh Hill: 'The residue of the Hugh Hill being a rockey, furzey and heathy peece of ground for the most part thereof and verrie barren; onely a small part thereof hath been inclosed for arable and a bowling alley, which said hill is the south west part of Maries Iland and almost devided from the residue of the said Iland by the sea almost meteing at the HughPort and Port Creso [Porth Cressa], haveing only a neck of land or rather of sand whereby they remaine conioyned, which said Hughhill conteine' by est. 120 ac., £13 6s 8d.

Rat Iland [Rat Island], 'near the Hugh and the Hugh harbor, which is a blockhouse for preservation of the said harbor unto which at low water they may pass on drye ground, but is of noe other vallue or use then afforesaid.'

Harbors: 'There are onely three harbors where ships maye ride safley in most wethers and these are called the Maryes harbor which is in Maries Sound neare Ratt Iland on the north the Hugh Hill and neare the maine of

Maries Iland; one other is in New Grimsbey Sound which lyes betweene the Ilands of Tresco and the Briars and is the best for ships of burthen; the other is in Old Grimsbye Sound which is one the east of Tresco Iland, in which said harbor everie alian payes for ancoridge two shillings sixpence and for sea breach twelve pence each, and everie English vessell payes for ancoridge fowre pence and for keyedge six pence. The proffitts of the harbor wee estimate', £6 13s 4d.

Shipwracks: 'The proffitts ariseing upon any shipwrack or other wracks cast away upon any of the said Ilands or the rocks lyeing neare the same doe belong to the Lord or Farmor of the said Ilands and Admirall of England for the time being and have been usually ceased by the Governors thereof. The customes of the wracks are that if any wracks bee found on shore by any of the inhabitants of the said Ilands, such persons are to have one third thereof or the vallue for salvadge and the residue to the lord or Farmer and Admirall of England for the time beeing according to theire customes, and if any wracks bee found floting then such inhabitants fynding the same and ceasing thereon is to have one half thereof or the vallue thereof . . . and the Lord or Farmor and the foresaid Admirall the rest. The Lord or Farmor of the said Ilands have power to hold Courts of Admiraltie within the said Ilands for the discoverie of all wracks and concealments of wrecks, all which said Admiraltye and the proffitts of the wrecks wee estimate to bee worth' on av. £6 13s 4d.

Fishing: 'There is an excellent fishing about the said Ilands for ling, cod and conger besides there fishing for lobsters and crab which hath been discontinued since the trobels; also besides theire fishing for other fish as mulletts, soles, place, salmon, peale mackrell, whiting, whiteing [sic], pullocks [pollock], the whistleing fish with abundance of other small fish which are of litle esteme by reason they have noe vent for the same. Which said fishing is for the most part managded by the Ilanders of the severall Ilands, all of them beeing bound upon theire severall tenements to sett out one fisher man from everye tenement, but the inhabitants have been much impoverished and wasted by the trobles and theire boates and fishing tackell much decayed and lost by the Pickeroones and other Pirates which doe much molest those Ilands and which hath much decayed there fishing of late. The custome of theire fishing is to sett out as many boats as they can man and tackle with fowere or five men in each boate, who begins theire fishing for ling, codd and conger about Maye daye and continue till Bartholmewday or thereabouts. These boates doe usually once a daye in the morneing for the most part bring all theire craft unto Ecles Port at St Maries Old Towne and deliver theire fish by number and measure according to an assize agreed on there unto a certaine officer appointed by the Lord Farmor or Governor of the Ilands called the Rockman, who dresses and stores up the said fish according to directions given him for the use of the Lord Farmor or Governor who hath them all at certaine rates and prises agreed on yearly according to custome and assize, and which said Rockman keeps an accompt thereof betweene the fishermen and the Lord or Farmor according to which accompt the fishermen are paid at the end of the fishing, alloweing on tenth part of all the said fish or the vallue thereof for a tyth unto the Lord Farmor or Governor, receiving the same according to custome. Besides this the said fisherman doe paye the tyth of all theire small fish that is of all other fish in kind as they dayly catch them with or besides these, except onely of such small fish as are taken for baites for theire greater fishing and of the overplus of such fish then taken. And also after Bartholmew Daye the fishermen have the disposeing of all fish they take payeing onely tyth of all in kind, the proffitt of which said fishing and the tyth thereof as it is received by the Lord Farmor or Governor of the said Ilands wee estimate to be worth' p.a. £100.

'All the inhabitants of the said island doe usually paye tyth corne in kinde, but in regard wee have returned the severall lands and tenements vallued to there best improvement at which they are or maye bee lett, therefore wee cannot put any value upon the said tyth but have comprehended the same in the vallue of the severall tenements as above said.'

'The severall tennants and inhabitants are by agreement to repaire theire tenements, to give accompt of all wracks, to grind theire corne at the mills afforesaid; also each tennant is to maintaine an able man with a muskitt and amunition to bee ready to serve for defence of the Ilands; also to keep and maintaine one able seamon with fishing craft to fish according to the custome afforesaid, and noe inhabitant to depart the ilands without leave first obteined of the Lord or his Farmor or Governor.'

'The severall tennants and farmors possessors of the severall lands and tenements in all the said ilands doe hold theire severall tenures eyther by lease from Mr Godolphin or Sir William Godolphin or els ad placitum.

There is a tynn myne in the said Iland which hath beene proved and found to bee of noe vallue or not of vallue to answer the charge in gaining thereof.'

Mr Godolphin's Claim

The islands, castles and tenements 'wee fynd claimed by Francis Godolphin and Sir William Godolphin for divers yeares yet to come and unexpired by vertue of an indenture tripartite under the Great Seale and Seale of the Admiraltye. A coppie of the originall thereof was produced unto us and attested . . . bearing date [10 Aug. 1603] betweene King James on the first part, Sir William Godolphin on the second part and Charles Earle of Nottingham, Lord Admirall of England on the third part, witnesseth that the said King James . . . grants unto the said Sir William, his executors and asignes all those iles, ilands territories and rocks' [their names follow] together with all lands, mines fisheries and 'the moyetie of all shipwracks . . . the other moyetie thereof to the Lord Admirall for the time beeing'; all liberties and 'full . . . authoritie . . . to heare and examine and finally to determine all plainties, suites, matters, accions . . . betwene partie and partie inhabiting within the said ilands . . . offences happening upon the seas belonging to the Court of Admiraltye allwaes excepted'. To hold from the expiry of a former grant by Queen Elizabeth and Edward Lord Clinton and Saye, Lord Admiral, to Francis Godolphin esq., dated 14 Dec. 1570 for 38 years, for a term of 50 years, paying £20 yearly to the Receiver of the Duchy of Cornwall.

'The said King James further covenanting that the said Sir William . . . shall and maye have and take everie yeare dureing the said terme at the

Kings price one last of gunpowder payeing ready monye for the same, also
that it may and shalbe lawfull for the said Sir William or his asignes to take
up and press his and theire owne tennants and servants to serve the King
under the said Sir William . . . at the onely charge of the said Sir William
within the said Ilands in time of warr for keeping and defending of the said
Ilands against the enemie, and also that it shalbe lawfull for the said Sir
William . . . soe often as need shall require to take up and provide in the
Kings name or in the name of his successors as well timber, wheat, malt as
any other victuals and provitions whatsoever at the Kings prises within the
Countie of Cornewall, payeing therefore readie monie for the same to be
used and imployed only within the said Iles, and also that the said Sir
William shall not sell this present lease not his terme therein . . . without
licence from the King or his successors nor dispose the same by his last will
and testament to any of his daughters unless shee bee maried to one of
yeares likely and meet to defend the same nor to any other within age.'
Enrolled 24 July [1604].

A grant made since July 1 1635
King Charles by indenture of 22 June 1636 granted to Francis Godolphin
esq. the lands and priviledges listed for 50 years at a rent £20 over and above
the previous rent, total £40.
Md. It is not known whether the lease of Queen Elizabeth was surrendered
or cancelled when the lease of King James was granted, 'therefore [we]
cannot sett downe the residue of the yeares yet to come and unexpired in the
last lease'.
Md. 'Wee conceave the grand consideracion upon which all the said leases
were granted was the preservation of the said Ilands from the enimye.'
Md. John St Aubine esq. claims part of the islands by virtue of a ninepart
indenture of 24 June 1568 between (1) Henry Champernone, (2) John
Danvers, (3) Richard Bowles esq., (4) Dame Margret Throgmorton, one of
the daughters and coheirs of Thomas Whittington esq., (5) Brice Berkly
esq. and Ann his w., another of the said coheirs, (6) John St Awbin and
Blanch his w., another d. and coheiress, (7) John Nanffan esq. and Alice his
w., another coheiress, (8) Henrie Poole esq., cousin and coheir, i.e. s. and
heir of Elizabeth, d. of said Whittington, (9) Roger Bodenham esq., tenant
by courtesy after the death of Jane his late w., another of the coheirs
witnessing 'that whereas suite had been depending betweene the said
Henrie Champernoone on the one part and all the residue before named on
the other parte about the Iles of Scillye . . . it is now covenanted and agreed
betweene the said parties [that] the said Champernoone for [£300] resignes
all his title therein unto the rest of the parties abovesaid to the severall uses
and purposes hereafter declared [namely] one third part of all the said Iles
of Syllye and other things in strife to the use of the said Sir John Danvers
and his heires for ever, one third part to Richard Bowles and his heires for
ever, and the other third part to the uses following viz. the said third part
beeing devided into six parts, one six part of the said third part to the use of
the said Dame Margret Throgmorton and her heires, one other sixt part to
the use of Brice Berkley and Ann his wife and one sixt part . . . to the use of
John Saintawbin and Blanch his wife . . . and the other sixt part to John
Nanfon and Alice his wife . . . and the other sixt part to Henrie Poole and his
heires and one other sixt part . . . unto Roger Bodman and his heires . . .

But the said Mr Saintawbon nor his father . . . hath been in possession of any the said Syllyes or of part of the same; therefore wee referr his claime to bee considered by the Honorable the Trustees and Surveyor Generall.' Md. 'The said Mr Saintawbin informes that all the residue of the coheires except his ancestors did pass awaye all theire title in the Syllyes unto Queene Elizabeth.

Reserved rent on the lease	£40
Total improved value	£990 9s 2d
Total acreage	3750 acres 1 rood

This Survey was presented [7 Sept. 1652] by us
John Fistze
Samuell Cottman
John Haddocke'

38   MANOR OF STOKE CLYMSLAND

DCO S/5; PRO E 317 (C)/40. An ancient manor of the Duchy. Its boundaries corresponded closely with those of Stoke Climsland parish. The manor is unique in preserving a demesne, even though it was leased, and in being divided into three tithings.

'A Survey of the Mannor of Stoke Clymsland . . . retorned [11 Jan. 1649/50]

DEMEANES IN HAND

All that parcell called Eneham [Inny Ham] heretofore in the possession of William Parker Clerke . . . but now in the Lord's hand and conteyneth by mensuracion [125 ac.] whereof there is [109 ac.] of arrable land, [9 ac.] of pasture ground and [7 ac.] of woodground' worth at an impr. val. £30. Woods on the premises now worth £2 5s.
'Alsoe the toll of the tinn mines within the said Mannor formerly in lease unto one Walter Adams but now in hand', worth p.a. £1 10s.
Woodland called Wareham [*id.*] Wood, previously held by John Harris esq. but now in the Lord's hand, by admeasurement' 182 ac. Impr. val. £26 12s. Trees and saplings, in number 2552 are worth 'in ready money as they there stand' £287 2s. Underwoods 'not cutt downe', 113 ac. and of 20 years' growth, worth £200.
'The said woode is bounded on the west, north and east with the River of Tamar and on the south with a certeine comon thereunto adioyninge, being parte of the said Mannor'.
'There is alsoe [69 ac.] of two yeares groweth' worth £18 8s. 'Allsoe all that . . . woodland called Greenescombe [Greenscoombe] Wood, formerly in the tenure of the said John Harris but now fallen into the Lords hands . . . by admeasurement [36 ac.] worth £3.
There are noe Timber Trees or Saplins groweing on the premisses. The Underwoods groweing in parte of the premisses of divers yeares groweth is worth in ready money £19 12s.
Md. 'Wee have not valued the herbage of the said wood because it is graunted unto the customary tennants.

Richard Langford claimeth to hold the fishery of the River of Enee [Inny] by the rent of [5s] but produced noe graunt for the same', worth £1 10s. Margl. notes by W. Webb: 'It matters not so long as the soyle is before valued. This grant to be produced. Vide the abstract of this grant of fishing entred on the backside of the sheete, and allowed by order of the Committee of Obstructions.'

On the dorse of memb. 2: 'Thomas Caldwall by virtue of a grant made to him [14 June 1628] of all that fishing in the River and waters of Enee and Tamar for . . . the terme of [31] yeares . . . under the yeerely rent of [5s, 16 Feb. 1631[1]] assigns all his right . . . unto Richard Langford. [sd.] William Webb [10 June 1652]'.

'DEMEANES IN LEASE'

Kerrybullocke [Kerrybullock] Parke: 'All those houses, buildings, meadows, feedeings, pastures and wood ground lying . . . within the walkes and circuits of the late disparked parke of Kerrybullocke . . . conteyninge by admeasurement [465 ac.] which is this distinguished':

3 parcels of meadow with an adjoining waste, 5 ac.;   8 parcels of pasture and feeding ground known as Farme Ground, 46 ac.;   Other pasture likewise divided, 90 ac.;   Pasture not divided, 196 ac.;   Wood ground of which 46 ac. are known as 'the Wood on the Farme Ground', 123 ac.

Within the Park are 'two open quarries, the one of stone, the other of slate, and one old house consisting of five roomes . . . knowen by the name of Lodge House and is now in greate decay.' Impr. val. £80.

Premises, woods and underwoods 'upon the Farme Ground' by estimate 46 ac., granted to Sir Richard Buller by L. P. of 28 March 1625; term, 99 years, on lives of John (36), Anthony (30) and William (dec.) sons of Richard B. Rent £6 and £2 for the wood. Excepted: 'one mill with a parcell of wood ground to the said mill belonging and the yearely rent of [4s]'. Also trees, woods, mines, quarries.

Conditions: to plant 12 trees yearly. No trees may be cut of less than 10 years' growth 'and then onely in time convenient for cuttinge of woode, and after every such cuttinge made to enclose and encopice with sufficient hedges and ditches the said woodes soe cutt and the same to preserve and keepe from biteing and hurteing and spoyling by beasts dureing the terme for that kinde of woode lymitted in the statute.' All 'bootes' allowed. 4556 trees now growing, worth £607 9s 8d.

'Underwood of 93 ac. reserved out of the said grant are with the foresaid woods of the Farme Ground sold by Francis Buller esq. this last yeare for £130 of which he is to be accountable for the said reserved woodes soe by him sould the some of' £94 10s.

The Park is now in the possession of Francis Buller and is 'bounded on the north with a lane leading from Stoke Clymsland to Mr Connockes fee farme mill called Treovis Mill and with the said mill and another lane leadeing thence unto Hingsdon [Hingston] Downe on the east, and soe by the said Downe on the south unto certeine lands of the customary tennants . . . and by the said lands on the west unto the lane aforesaid'.

[1] Legible only Duchy copy of Survey.

FREEHOLDERS OF THE MANOR

John Connocke esq. 'holdeth freely to himself and his heires for ever' a ten. called Beiles [Beals] and 100 ac. in 1½ ac. C. 'by the service of gathering the Lord's rent yearely and suite to the Lords courtes every three weekes'. Relief, according to custom. This service is valued to be worth p.a. £2.

id.: ten. called Knathan [Gnatham] and 45 ac. in 3 farl., rent 2s 6d.

id.: ten. called Dighouse alias Honessa [Dighouse] and 67½ ac. in 1½ farl., rent 2s 6d.

id.: ten. called North Alston alias Alston [North Alston] and 45 ac. in 3 farl., rent 2s 6d.

Pierce Mannaton esq.: ten. called Combesheade [West Coombeshead] and 45 ac. in 3 farl., rent 2s 6d.

Heirs of Sampson Manaton esq. viz. Francis M., Joyce Thomas, Judith M. and Elizabeth M.: mess. called North Horton [Norton] and 30 ac. in ½ ac. C., rent 2s 6d.

id.: mess. in Nether Hammett [Lower Hampt] and 30 ac. in ½ ac. C., rent 1s 8d.

Heirs of Nicholas Leach esq.: mess. called Pempithe [Pempwell?] and 15 ac. in 1 farl., rent 10d.

id.: mess. in South Horton and 30 ac. in ½ ac. C., rent 1s 8d.

Edward Phillipps gt.: mess. in Nether Hamet and 45 ac. in 3 farl., rent 2s 6d.

Heirs of Sampson Mannaton, as above: mess. and ten. called Mannaton the Over and Mannaton the Nether [Manaton in South Hill] and 120 ac. in 2 ac. C., rent 13s 4d.

Thomas Wills: mess. called South Whetford [Whiteford] and 45 ac. in 3 farl., rent 2s 6d.

Lewis Hatch: mess. called Hatche [Hatch] and 45 ac. in 3 farl., rent 2s 6d.

Robert Couch: mess. in South Norton and 30 ac. in ½ ac. C., rent 1s 8d.

George Jackeman: mess. called Borrington [Burraton] and 15 ac. in 1 farl., rent 1s 3d.

Sampson Brent: mess. in Barraton and 15 ac. in 1 farl., rent 1s 3d.

Anthony Mannaton: the mill called Manaton Mill. Suit only.

Robert Woode: certain lands formerly held by one Reede, 1s 3d.

John Hawton sn.: certain lands, relief, suit and service only.

Total quite rents   £4 3s 9d

'Fee Farme Mill within the said Mannor
Benedict of Bxlexe [sic] by writeing in manner of a chirographe made and sealed in the reigne of Edward the Third by Edmond then Earle of Cornewall[2] hath made and graunted unto him and his heires all that farme mill of the Onesse [Treovis] within the Mannor of Climstone alias Climsland with the liberty of grinding and all appurtenances thereof [rendering yearly to the Earl] foure markes of silver [two at Michaelmas and 2 at Easter] . . . furthermore it is graunted by the said writeing to the said Benedict that it shall and may be lawfull for him to erect and build the said mill destroyed in the reigne of King Stephen at his will and pleasure and the said mills to have and to hold as of right is accustomed for the foresaid rent . . . if the said rent . . . shold be unpaid . . . or the said mills shold be destroyed that then the

---

[2] Earl Edmund died in 1300. Clearly Edward I was meant.

said lands and tenements shold be forfeited for ever.' John Connocke has possession of the mills by virtue of his marriage to the heir of one Beile 'whoe had the same from his ancestors that held it by the said grant.'

HANT TYTHING
CONVENTIONARY TENANTS OF INHERITANCE

	Fine	Rent	Barbage rent[3]
John Letheby, Joan Fudge and George Fudge: mess. in Byanleighe and 16 ac. in 1 farl.	34s	2s 6d	nil
Joan Fudge: 'one bloweing mill lately built on three rodes of wast land'	nil	8d	nil
George Fudge: 3 roods of waste 'in three Byhanheijs nigh Bianleigh forde'	3d	1d	nil
Robert Marten: moiety of ten. and 20 ac. in Trelane [*id.*]; John Letheby: the other moiety	42 s 6d	3s	1s 4d
Joan Bromlein: 'one house in Trelane conteyninge in length sixtie feete in breadth twenty seven	2s	4d	nil
Richard Tooker: 'one fulling mill there'	2d	1s 8d	nil
John Lithby, Bartholomew Trees and Joan Brookein: ten. called Trealbis [Treovis] and 34 ac.	29s 4d	2s 4d	1s 4d
John Dodge gt.: ten. in Tuesse alias Mogberie and 8 ac. except a house and garden; Richard Gressam: the said house and garden	16s	1s 4d	nil
John Dodge: ten. in Turvars and 16 ac.	20s 6d	2s 8d	nil
id.: house and garden in Turvars	21s	3s 4d	nil
id.: moiety of ten. and 8 ac. in Cottersland John Letheby: the other moiety	10s	1s 4d	nil
John Cornew: ten and 16 ac. in Lidwell [*id.*]	24s	2s 8d	nil
Katherin Hawton: ten. and 16 ac. there	24s 4d	2s 9½d	nil
Robert Martin, William Chubb, Ezra Triggs and Sampson Jackeman: ten. in Lidwell and 32 ac.	43s 4d	5s 4½d	nil
John Dodge, William Thomas, Sampson Giddy, Richard Leache, Katherin Hawton and William Wroth: ten. in Lidwell and 8 ac.	11s	1s 4½d	nil
John Cornew: ten. and 32 ac. in Lidwell	34s	4s	nil
Francis Jope gt.: mess. and 32 ac. there	29s	4s 2d	nil
Stephen Bant, John Jory, Thomas Smalley, Leonard Williams and John Letheby: ten. called Kelly alias Kelple [Kellybray] and 19 ac.	15s	1s 8d	8d

[3] Possibly a rent for grazing sheep. See J. Hatcher, *Rural Economy in Duchy of Cornwall* (1970), pp. 68–9.

	Fine		Rent		Barbage rent[3]	
Richard Dodge: ten. in Clymstone Cockingtone [Cockington] and 22 ac.	30s		6s	8d	4d	
id.: and John Cornew: ten. there and 13 ac.	20s		2s		4d	
George Harrey, Nicholas Brooke and Honor Barbor, John Smyth and Robert Hatche: ten. there and 24 ac.	23s		3s		nil	
Francis Jope gt.: ten. in Mearefield [Mearfield] and 32 ac.	24s	10d	4s		nil	
id.: a piece of ground there of 16 perches		10d		4d	nil	
John Cornew, Joan Collin and William Chubb: ten. in Cleve and 12 ac.	18s	4d	1s	6d	nil	
Richard Dodge, Sampson Grills, Joan Collin and Robert Knight: ten. there and 32 ac.	53s	4d	2s	8d	1s	
Richard Dodge and Sampson Grills: 2 ten. in Stoke [Stoke Climsland]	21s		1s		nil	
Walter Horrell, John Letheby, Sampson Hawkin, Robert Couch and Sampson Skinner: ten. in Stoke and 21 ac.	35s	4d	3s	4d	nil	
Tristram Clerke: 'one shopp by the Church Centry in Stoke		nil		6d	nil	
Tristram Bowhey: house and garden in Stoke		4d	1s	8d	nil	
Robert Knight: ten. in Alreyne [Alren] and 16 ac.	17s	8d	2s	4d	1s	4d
Robert Knight, John Wills, Mary Wills, Robert Bowhey, John Crappe, John Lethey and Richard Hatche: ten. in Alreyn and 26 ac.	21s		3s		1s	4d
Sampson Grills and John Hewett: ten. called Bitheway and 34 ac.	36s	8d	3s	8d	1s	4d
Sampson Sleighman and John Crappe: ten. in Southcombe [South Coombe] and 17 ac	30s		1s	6d	8d	
Joan Marrett, Sampson Jackeman, Robert Bruen, Elizabeth Bennett and Ezekiell Collins: ten. in Southcombe and 36 ac.	42s		3s	8d	1s	4d
John Hewett, Thomas Jewell and Ezekiell Collins: ten. there and 32 ac.	36s		3s	6d	1s	4d
Sampson Grills and John Hewett: ten. there and 18 ac.	44s		2s	8d	1s	4d
George Chubb and Elenor Crabb: ten. in Knockett [Crocket] and 18 ac.[4]	23s	1d	3s	6d	nil	
Edward Bowhey: ten. there and 16 ac.	19s		1s	8d	nil	
Mathew Betle, John Wescott and John Crift: ten. there and 18 ac.	21s		2s		nil	
Edward Bowhey: 'one fulling mill and one knocking mill in Knockett'	6s	8d	6s	8d	nil	
Robert Knight: ten. and 18 ac. there	16s		2s		1s	4d

[4] Order different in PRO copy.

WESTLAND TYTHING: CONVENTIONARY TENNANTS

	Fine	Rent	Barbage rent[3]
Edward Bowhey, John B., John Croft and Henry Grubb: 1 rood and 10 perches of land, called a 'landyoke',[5] in Hurledowne	3d	1d	nil
Edward Bowhey and Henry Grills: 33 ac. in ½ ac. C. in Hurledowne	16s	3s 4d	nil
John Bowhey, John Croft and Henry Grubb: ten. there and 32 ac.	7s	3s 4d	1s 4d
George Harvey, John Masters, Mathew Beile, Nicholas Jefford, Roger Combe, Elizabeth Dodge and Mathew Dodge: ten. called Dena alias Dene and 32 ac.	15s	4s 4d	nil
Robert Reade and John Master: ten. in Kilberry and 32 ac.	28s	3s 4d	1s 4d
John Dodge, Robert Combe and Roger Clerke: ten. there and 32 ac.	32s 8d	3s 4d	1s 4d
John Brent: ten. and 32 ac. there	38s 6d	3s 4d	1s 4d
Robert Jackeman: ten. and 32 ac. in Whitford	40s	4s	1s 4d
Sampson Heale, Stephen Clerke, Robert Clerke, John Clerke and George Jackeman: ten. and 48 ac. there	66s 8d	5s 4d	2s 8d
Robert Jackman and Elizabeth Crabb: ten. and 8 ac. in 1 farl. in Whiteford [*id.*]	11s 8d	1s 2d	8d
George Jackeman: ten. and 16 ac. in 1 farl. there	11s	1s	nil
Sampson Heale and Robert Jackeman: ten. and 8 ac. in 1 farl. in Whiteford	13s 4d	1s 6d	8d
S. H. [sic], Margarett Hawton and Elizabeth Crabb: ten. and 17 ac. in Whiteford	11s	1s	8d
Margarett Hawton: ten. and 8 ac. in 1 farl there	13s 4d	1s 4d	8d
George Litheby: ten. and 16 ac. in ½ ac. C.	23s 4d	3s 1d	nil
Edward Bowhey and Sampson Heale: ten. and 32 ac. in ½ ac. C. in Whiteford	33s 4d	2s 6d	1s 8d
Walter Gill and Thomas Giddy: ten. in Combesheade and 32 ac. in ½ ac. C.	39s 8d	2s 8d	1s 4d
Thomas Giddy and Walter Gill: 1 ac. of waste in Combesheade	3d	2d	nil
Sampson Brent: ten. and 32 ac. in ½ ac. C. there	39s 4d	2s 10d	1s 4d
Anthony Grubb: ten. in Polhilza [Polhilsa] and 15 ac. in 1 farl.	27s 4d	2s 8d	8d
Henry Grills and Theobald G.: ten. in Polhilza and 46 ac. in 3 farl.	15s	3s 2d	1s 4d

[5] A *landyoke* would appear to have been an intake or enclosure from the waste. It was divided into small parcels, held presumably by those who reclaimed it.

	Fine	Rent	Barbage rent[3]
Richard Grubb, Joan Killigrew, Joan Adams and Mathew Bligh: ten. and 32 ac. in ½ ac. C.	41s	3s 2d	1s 4d
Sampson Treasse: mess. in Cockington and 46 ac. in 3 farl.	53s 4d	4s 8d	2s
id.: ten. and 20 ac. in ½ ac. C. in Cockington	30s	2s 9d	1s 4d
Tristram Brent: ½ ac. of meadow in a landyoke in Whitecroft	5s	4d	nil
Sampson Treasse and Roger Clerke: 4 ac. of waste in Whitecroft	4s	4d	nil
Sampson Treasse and William Hatch: ten. and 32 ac. in ½ ac. C. in Pitt	36s 8d	4s	8d
Thomas Giddy and Henry Grills: ten. and 20 ac. in Baraton	29s	3s 4d	8d
Thomas Giddy: ten. and 20 ac. there	28s	3s	2½d
George Jackeman: 16 ac. in 1 landyoke in Geresland and Baraton	3s 4d	1s 4d	nil
Pierce Mannaton and George Jackeman: ten. and 30 ac. in ½ ac. C. in Baraton	25s 4d	2s 6d	1s 4d
Adam Grills: ten. and 24 ac. in Baraton	33s 4d	4s	8d
Thomas Geddy: 2 ac. in 1 landyoke in Baraton	6d	4d	nil
id.: ten. and 41 ac. in 3 farl. in Baraton	54s 4d	4s 4d	1s 4d
Elizabeth Stephens and William Sheere: ten. called Keniscombe in Linkinhorne (Kingscoombe) and 32 ac. in ½ ac. C.	nil	6s 8d	nil
Pierce Mannaton esq.: ten. called Torre [Torr] and 24 ac. in ½ ac. C.	28s	3s 4d	1s 4d
id.: ten. called Toggehill and 14 ac. in 1 farl.	8s 6d	2s	nil
Sampson Mathew and George M.: ten. and 27 ac. in ½ ac. C. in Fenterdon [Venterdon]	38s	2s 6d	1s 4d
John Hawton sn. and John H. jn.: ten. and 24 ac. in ½ ac. C. in Fenterdon	36s	3s 2d	1s 4d
Bennett Couch and William Trease: ten. and 24 ac. there in ½ ac. C.	32s	2s 6d	1s 4d
John Hawton, John Letheby, Mathew Letheby and Sampson Mathewes: ten. and 32 ac. in ½ ac. C. in Fenterdon	37s	2s 4d	1s 4d
Stephen Hunn, William Bowhey, Ambrose Mannaton, John Dodge and Richard Parmiter: ten. and 32 ac. in 3 farl. in Kingstone [Kingston]	43s 4d	4s 8d	1s 4d
Robert Knight and William Warren: ten. and 28 ac. in ½ ac. C. Kingstone	40s	3s 4d	1s 4d
Dorothy Jewell and John J.: ten. and 18 ac. in 1 farl. there	16s	2s 4d	1s 4d

	Fine	Rent	Barbage rent
Abell Dickson, Nathaniell Mivord and Dorothy Fathers: ten. and 32 ac. in ½ ac. C. there	33s	2s 8d	1s 4d
Beaton Lampen, Daniell Sergeant, Elinor Adams, Mary Marrett and Robert Doble: mess. in Burg Well and 16 ac.	nil	5s	nil

NORDON TYTHING

	Fine	Rent	Barbage rent
William Picke, John Darley, Robert Cundy, Robert Marten, George Hawkin and the overseers of the poor of the Parish of Stoke Clymsland: ten. and 19 ac. in ½ ac. C. and 4 ac. of waste in 1 landyoke in Whille	35s 4d	3s 4d	1s 4d
John Masters, Richard Beile, Oliver Pellow, Alice Hawton, William Pawley and Jane Wewill: ten. in Northdon [North Down] and 32 ac. in ½ ac. C.	43s 6d	3s 4d	8d
Margarett Chubb alias Giddy and John Masters: ten. and 30 ac. in ½ ac. C. in Northdon	46s 8d	4s 6d	8d
John Aunger, Tristram Cundy, Anthony Masters, John Moncke, Peter Symons and John Masters: ten. and 50 ac. in ½ ac. C. and 2 farl. in Northdon	20s	5s 4d	nil
Richard Sergeant, Richard Gest and John Masters jn.: ten. and 32 ac. in ½ ac. C. in Northdon	35s	2s 8d	8d
Nicholas Beile: 14 ac. of waste in 1 farl in Northdon	5s	1s 4d	nil
William Cliverton, John Chubb, Richard Short, Walter Horrell and Nicholas Brooke: ten. in Turnley alias Oldclyms [Oldclims] and 32 ac. in ½ ac. C.	24s	2s 4d	1s 4d
John Smith gt.: ten. and 32 ac. in ½ ac. C. in Turley	49s	4s	1s 4d
Anthony Moncke: ten. and 32 ac. there	39s	4s 1d	1s 4d
John Chubb, George Letheby, Philip Cleverton, John Cornew and Sampson Giddy: ten. and 28 ac. in ½ ac. C. there	28s	3s 8d	1s 4d
Anthony Moncke: ten in Pempell [Pempwell] and 8 ac. in 1 farl.	20s	1s 4d	nil
Richard Short: ten. and 16 ac. in 1 farl. there	19s	2s	8d
John Smith gt.: ten. and 18 ac. in ½ ac. C. there	24s	2s 4d	1s 4d
William Gliddon: ten. and 32 ac. in ½ ac. C. in Dovehouse alias Penhale [Downhouse?]	2s	3s 6d	1s 4d
id.: ten. and 16 ac. in 1 farl. there	10s	2s 4d	nil

	Fine	Rent	Barbage rent
Nicholas Lampen and Thomas Parson: ten. and 20 ac. in 1 farl. there	13s	2s 8d	nil
William Treasse and John Smyth: ten. and 32 ac. in ½ ac. C. there	20s	3s 6d	1s 4d
Nicholas Lampen, John Joppe, William Cleverton, George Hawton, Downes Joppe and John Smyth gt.: ten. called Holy Well and 70 ac. in 1 ac. C.	93s 4d	6s 10d	2s 8d
William Bowhey, Thomas Parsons and Agatha Hunn: ten. called Updowne and 32 ac. in ½ ac. C.	29s	3s	1s 4d
Richard Hawkin and George Joppe: ten. and 32 ac. in ½ ac. C. in Alrestone	34s 4d	4s	1s 4d
Tristram Hatche: ten. in Helle and 32 ac. in ½ ac. C., and the seventh part of a land-yoke being 30 ac. by estimation of waste land	22s	1s 3d	1s 4d
Richard Hawkin: ten. in Helle and 32 ac. in ½ ac. C. and a seventh of a landyoke containing 30 ac.	22s	1s 3d	nil
Nicholas Bevile, Henry Wolcott, Richard Sliman, Robert Woode, Sampson Hawkin and William Shorte: ten. in Tudwell [Tutwell] and 21 ac in ½ ac. C.	27s 4d	2s 4d	1s 4d
Sampson Hunn, Nicholas Beyle and Henry Wolcott: ten. there and 22 ac. in ½ ac. C. of waste and a seventh of 32 ac. of waste	50s 4d	2s 2d	8d
Dewnes Joppe, Daniell Clerke, Joan Prater, Samuell Hatche and Sampson Geddy: ten. and 16 ac. in ½ ac. C. and a seventh of a landyoke containing 22 ac.	23s	3s 3d	8d
Anthony Moncke and Sampson Hunn: 1 farl. in Oxenbury Downe	3s	1s 10d	nil
William Gliddon: 2 ac. of waste in a land-yoke in Oxenbury Downe	1s	3d	nil
Willian Cleverton and John Chubb: 12 ac. of waste in a landyoke called Oldidiate or Olidiate	2s	6d	nil
William Gliddon and George Harvey: a piece of waste of 16 ac. there	4s	5d	nil
John Geddy and other tenants of the Manor: 16 ac. of waste in 2 landyokes in Eneham Downe	1s	1s 10½d	nil
'There is one corne mill formerly a blowing mill, late in the possession of Peter Corrington'	30s	10s	nil
John Masters: ten. in Dunstone and 32 ac. in ½ ac. C.	10s	2s 8d	nil

	Fine	Rent	Barbage rent
Robert Jackeman: ½ ac. of moore ground in Broadmore	6d	6d	nil
John William and Robert Knight: 3 ac. of waste in a landyoke in Broadmore	1s	3d	nil
Assigns of Richard Bennett: ½ farl. in Knightford alias Kneeford	1s	6d	nil
Sampson Grills: 2 ac. of waste in a landyoke in Hoggeslidiate	6d	2d	nil
Sampson Brent: ten. in Westhurledowne and 32 ac. of waste	4s	2s 4d	nil
id.: 12 ac. there in a landyoke	8d	10d	nil
Tristram Beale: ten. there and 38 ac. in 3 farl.	9s	2s 6d	nil
Walter Gill: 1 ac. of waste there	3d	1d	nil
Assigns of William Hunn and others: 6 ac. of waste in Roughdowne	4s	1s	nil
Assigns of Joan Drowne and others: 32 ac. of waste in Roughdowne	4s	1s	nil
Assigns of William Hunn: 2 landyokes there	1s	3d	nil
Richard Short, Sampson Hunn, Nicholas Beale and Dewnes Joppe: 16 ac. of waste in Gonhoke [Gunoak]	4s	1s 4d	nil
Sampson Hunn: 1 ac. of waste there	nil	1s	nil
John Masters and John Smyth: ten. and 32 ac. in ½ ac. C. in Trecombe [*id.*]	16s	3s 4d	nil
William Bowhey, Robert Woode, Thomas Bennett, George Moncke, Richard Sergeant and Sampson Hunn: 32 ac. in Trecombe	16s	3s 4d	nil
Assigns of John Trease: 'one Cockrode'[6] in the foresaid tithing	nil	3d	nil
Assigns of Agatha Spoore: another cockrode	nil	3d	nil
Mr Dier gt.: a cockrode	nil	3d	
John Connocke esq.: another cockrode	nil	3d	nil
Assigns of John Joppe: a cockrode	nil	3d	nil
Assigns of Thomas Earle: 8 ac. in a landyoke	nil	8d	nil
Sampson Hunne: 16 ac. of waste in Kitweldowne	4s 6d	11d	nil
Robert Couch: 16 ac. of waste in Colemanscombe	6s 6d	2s 6d	nil
John Connocke esq.: 16 ac. of waste in Warewell Downe	6s 6d	2s	nil
William Smythe: a piece of land called Cleves in Blyndwell of 1 ac.	nil	6d	nil
Assigns of Richard Marten: waste ground called Poundfold Greene of 1 ac.	nil	2s	nil

[6] A *cockrode* is an elusive term. Mr Leslie Douch suggests that the word is 'cock-rood' or 'cock-loft', perhaps a garret or minor structure. The rent of three pence suggests something of low value.

	Fine	Rent	Barbage rent
All tenants: the pasture of Robinsland 'with the digging of stones there, alsoe the pasture of Hingsdon Downe or Comon, the pasture of Greenescombe, Sherwell and Hocke'	1s	17s 4d	nil
John Connocke esq.: 'one fulling mill with a streame of water there unto belonginge'	1s	3s 4d	nil
Assigns of Henry Masters: 'certeine cow-pastures called Smallycombe bying between Eneham Downe and North-downe' in all 6 ac.	1s	6d	nil
The overseers of the poor of the Parish of Stoke: a piece of waste ground near the Centery gate	nil	1s	nil
Sampson Hunn, Samuel Hatche, John Letheby, Mary Young, Richard Sleman, Richard Hutton, Katherin Stronte, Auguston Mouncke: ten. in Underhill and 32 ac. in $\frac{1}{2}$ ac. C. and a landyoke containing a seventh part of 32 ac.	20s	2s 10d	1s 4d
Elizabeth Crabb, Katherin Jeffrey, Sampson Trease and William Dickson: 24 ac. of waste in Mallettdowne [Tremollet Down]	13s 4d	1s 4d	nil
Thomas Geddy: 21 ac. in a landyoke	5s	1s 6d	nil
Assigns of John Harris esq.: 'one bloweing mill with an acre of woodground to the same belonging lying in the parke of Kerrybullocke'	nil	4s 5d	nil

A tabulated rental of (1) free tenants, (2) conventionary tenants.

'THE BOUNDES OF THE SAID MANNOR

The said Mannor is bounded on the north by the River of Ennee [Inny], on the north east by the River of Tamer, on the east by a certeine little lake called Grinscombe Lake [Greenscoombe brook] runninge into the said River of Tamer betweene the parishes of Stoke and Calstocke, and from thence unto a place called Shevill Heade [Higher Sherwill] in the south east betweene the said parishes, from thence unto Seven Stones [Sevenstones] in the south betweene the foresaid parishes; from thence to the comon way called the T . . . Way; from thence to a certeine place called Smalecombe from thence to Killibray [Kelly Bray] Corner on the south west, and so from thence as the high way leadeth towards the west betweene the Downe called Hurledowne and a certeine village called Meaders unto the said River of Enne where it first began.

Commons claimed by the Tennants of the said Mannor: The said tennants claime right of comon in Hings Downe [Hingston] by theire custome and that without stinte. Some of them soe alsoe claime right of comon in

Enneham and Wareham Woodes. Butt wee finde by auntient recod that the Lords of the said Mannor have time out of minde lett the said woodes and woodgrounds by leasse and the leasses have enioyed the possession thereof whereby it appeares that the said tennants have no interest or right of common in the foresaid woodes and woodgrounds but at the Lords pleasure.'

Customs of the Manor

A three weekly court is held 'at which all matters of difference betweene the tennants except felony and treason are tried and determined'.

The law [leet] courts are held yearly, at one of which a Reeve is chosen, whose duties are to collect fines, heriots, etc. The Reeve 'claimeth by custome to have the herriots . . . in kinde att such price as they are apprised at by two men sworne for the apprisement thereof.' Out of the money realised the Reeve 'is to finde the Steward and one more with him theire dinners every courte day; all which doe amount unto' on average £7 7s 8d. The Reeve is to appoint two men to collect the rent and barbage rent, 'which said collectors are to make good the fines and barbage rent ariseing out of the said Mannor notwithstanding any decrement thereof.'

Three tithing men are also to be chosen, who are sworne to execute 'the place of tithing-men for the severall tithings whereout they are chosen'.

An Assessions Court is held every seven years; its purpose (see page 000). The fine payable by each tenement 'is certeine and not to be encreased and which with the said New Knowledge money cones to' on average £25 8s 2d.

A relief is due from each free tenant on death or alienation, and from each customary tenant a best beast as a heriot, 'and although such tennant die seized of divers tenements or partes of tenements yett is there but onely one heriott due'.

Tenants may 'sett out [let] any part of their tenements with licence of the Steward'. The widows of customary tenents may continue to hold their late husbands' tenements during their widowhood.

Conventionary tenants are to pay to the Lord the sum of £6 within six years after each Assessions. This is called Old Knowledge Money and is worth on average 17s 1d and a seventh of 5d.

An Abstract of the Present Rents and future Improvements of the Manor

Rents of assize and perquisites	£30 4s
Barbage rent	£3 16s 2d
Old recognition money, on average	17s 1d
	and a seventh of 5d
Fines and tallage with New Recognition Money	£25 8s 2d
Demesne in possession valued at	£60 4d
Rents reserved upon lease	£8 5s
Toll of tin mines, on average	£1 10s
Rent of the fee farm mill	£2 13s 4d
Total	£132 13s 4d
	and a seventh of 5d
Improved valued of lands and fishing in lease	£81 10s
Woods, underwoods and timber trees are worth	£616 8s 8d

Md. 'Wee have not sett downe the ninety foure pounds tenn shillings [which Francis Buller esq. is to be accountable for] in the last mentioned some.'

This is an exact survey . . . (sd.)

39   MANOR OF STRATTON SANCTUARY

DCO S/4; PRO E 317 (C)/41. This very small manor lay in Stratton parish, close to the parish church, with one small tenement in Poughill parish. It belonged to Launceston Priory, and was acquired by the Duchy in 1540.

'A Survey of the Mannor of Stratton Sanctuary . . . retorned [4 July 1650].

FREEHOLDERS

John Lord Roberts, Barron of Truro holdeth freely to him and his heires for ever in soccage certeine lands for which he doth onely suite to the Lords courtes.'

[—] Gilbert gt.: certain lands	4d
Feoffees of Ockhampton: certain lands	3s
[—] Warmington gt.: certain lands	3s
Nicholas Paine: certain lands	1s
Robert Saunders and Oliver Yeo: divers messuages and tenements	15s
Total	£1 2s 4d

LEASEHOLDERS OF THE MANOR

Nicholas Paine of Stratton yeoman, by L. P. of 30 Nov. 1627, ten. in Stratton of 7¼ ac. 'divided into severall closes' namely: a meadow called East Sanctuary of 1 ac.; pasture called Midle Sanctuary of 3¼ ac.; pasture arable [sic] called West Sanctuary of 3 ac.; land called Orchard, 1 ac. Term: 99 years on the lives of Grace P. (40) w. of Nicholas P., Grace Downe (28) d. of Thomas Downe de Stratton, and Thomas Bullocke (dec.) s. of Robert B. Fine, at the Lord's will. Heriot 20s. Rent 16s. Impr. val. £10. Exceptions, etc.; to plant 4 trees yearly.

Thomas Downe, by indenture of 15 July 1622, ten. with 2 gardens and an orchard 'devided into six severall closes' of 13 ac. in all in Stratton. Term: lives of Anthony (36), Marke (32) and Grace (28) sons and d. of Thomas D. Fine, as above. Heriot 26s 8d. Rent 26s 8d. Impr. val. £12. Exceptions, etc.; to plant 2 trees yearly.
Md. Samuel Geare, merchant, has possession by virtue of his marriage to Grace D.

Jane Yeo wid., by L. P. of 30 Nov. 1627, ten. in Stratton with mess. and an orchard of 1 ac.; pasture called North Sanctuary of 3 ac.; pasture called Midle Sanctuary of 3¾ ac.; pasture called South Sanctuary of 4¼ ac. Term: 99 years on lives of Avery Yeo (dec.), Mary Deeme (32) and Isett Deeme (30) d. of John Deeme of Stratton. Fine, as above. Heriot 13s 4d. Rent 16s 6d. Impr. val £8. Exceptions, etc.; to plant 4 trees yearly.

William Warmington of Poughill, by indenture of 15 July 1622, ten. and dove house called Crabb in Poughill, with arable, meadow and pasture divided into several closes, in all 37 ac. Term: lives of George (46), Robert (44) and John (38), sons of William W. Fine, as above. Heriot 50s. Rent 24s. Impr. val. £40. Exceptions, etc.; to plant 3 trees yearly.

John Deeme, by L. P. of 2 June 1627, ten. in Stratton of 6 ac., namely a mess. and orchard of 1 ac., meadow of 2½ ac., a pasture called Midle Sanctuary of 1¼ ac., a pasture called East Sanctuary of 1½ ac. Term: 99 years on lives of John D. (dec.), John Avery (30) and Grace A. (26) s. and d. of John A. of Stratton Glewer. Fine: as above. Heriot £3. Rent 16s 8d. Impr. val. £9 10s. Exceptions, etc.; to plant 4 trees yearly.

Richard Barron of Stratton, by L. P. of 2 June 1627, ten. in Stratton of 7 ac. namely a mess. and orchard of 2 ac., a meadow called West Sanctuary of 1¼ ac.; a pasture called Midle Sanctuary of 1¼ ac., a pasture called East Sanctuary of 2½ ac. Term: 99 years, on the lives of Richard B. (not given), Elizabeth (44) his w. and John (34) [sic] their s. Fine, as above. Heriot £3. Rent 16s 8d. Impr. val. £11. Exceptions, etc.; to plant 4 trees yearly.

Sir John Walter, Sir James Fullerton and Sir Thomas Trevor, by L. P. of 14 June 1628, in trust and for the use of the late King, ten. of 1 ac. in Stratton. Term: 31 years. Fine, as above. Rent 8s. Impr. val. 32s.
Lease assigned 17 March 1628 to Richard Langford de Boyton, who assigned it by indenture of 10 Aug. 1634 to Lawrence Robinson of Stratton, cordwainer. Francis Porter clerk, is in possession by virtue of his marriage to the d. of Lawrence R.

'THE BOUNDS OF THE SAID MANNOR

This Mannor is bounded on the south side with a lane called Watery Lane from the house of Nicholas Paine unto a certeine village called Duddies [Diddies in Stratton], thence on the east by a certeine wood called Herparke Wood unto a village called Newley [New Leigh in Launcells] thence on the north by a little river of water unto a high way that leadeth from Norton to Stratton and thence by the said land on the west unto the towne of Stratton to the place where it began.'
Md. 'that there is one tenement in the parish of Poughill called Crabb which is intire of it selfe, noe other lands beinge intermixed therewith, and is now in the possession of William Warmington'.

CUSTOMS

Two courts leet and two courts baron are held yearly. A reeve is chosen at one of them to collect rents and perquisites, which amount on average to 10s.

ABSTRACT

Rents of assize and perquisites	£1 10s 4d
Rents of leaseholders	£6 8s 6d
Total	£7 18s 10d
Improved value of leasehold tenements	£92 2s

'This is an Exact Survey . . .'

40   MANOR OF TALSKIDY

DCO S/6; PRO E 317 (C)/42. This ancient manor of the Duchy formed a compact area within the parish of St Columb Major. It is noteworthy in never having had either demesne or free tenants.

'A Survey of the Mannor of Talskidy . . . retorned [3 April 1650].

There is noe demeasnese land neither are there any free tennants within this Mannor but conventionary tennants of inheritance onely'. They are as follows:

Mary Vivian wid., 'in free conventionary from seven yeares to seaven yeares dureing her widowhood', a ten. and the moiety of another, rent 18s 7½d;   Peter Jenkyn esq.: moiety of the above, except a house and garden, 4s 2½d;   Walter Vivian: ten. except the house and garden, 10s 5d;   William Vivian: moiety of ten. except⅛ and a house and garden, 6s 10½d;   Elizabeth Merrifield wid.: moiety of a ten., 6s 2½d;   Richard Merrifield: moiety of a ten., 6s 2½d;   Richard Duggoe: moiety of a ten., 6s 2½d;   Alice Rescorla wid.: ⅛ of a moiety of a ten., 1s 2d;   Thomas Richards: ¾ of a ten. and ⅛ of ⅛ of a moiety of a ten., 8s 7d;   Thomas Keslecke: ¼ of a ten. and a house and garden, 6s.

Total   £3 15s 6d.

'There is paid by the tennants for the first six yeares after every Assessions' £3 as a fine. Average 8s 6¾d and a seventh part of ¼d.
Old recognition money paid for the first three years after every Assessions 6s. Average 10¼d and a seventh part of ½d.
Perquisites, on average 6s 8d.

Total   £4 10s 6¾d and a seventh part of ¾d.

Bounds: 'on the north with Rosedenecke [Rosedinnick], on the south with Trewon [Trewan], on the east with Glivean and on the west with Trenowith [*id.*] being all the lands of John Vivian esq.'

CUSTOMS: No courts are kept since there are no free tenants; only the seven yearly Assessions court. The tenants perform the duties of Reeve. Tenants may surrender any part of their customary lands to any person at any time. A best beast is payable as heriot by the tenants. Widows may occupy their late husband's tenement until death or remarriage.

'This is an exact survey . . .'

41   MANOR OF TEWINGTON

DCO C/5; PRO E 317 (C)/43. This was an ancient manor of the Duchy, occupying a large but compact area in the south of the parish of St Austell. 'Tewington' is not a surviving place-name, and is now represented by 'Towan' the name of a farmstead on the western side of the manor.

'A Survey of the Mannor of Tewington . . . retorned [10 May 1650].

There is a peece of woodground conteyninge by estimacion 16 acres within a customary tenement of Oliver Saules esq., the herbage and underweedeing whereof is claimed by the said Mr Saule as parte of his said tenement for which he payeth a speciall rent of 8s per annum, which said woode was sould in the time of the warres to the said Oliver Saule for £3 an acre, and is worth at an improved value communibus annis 53s 4d.

The wood now groweing thereon being of about 3 yeares growth is valued to be worth £8.

FREE-TENNANTS OF THE SAID MANNOR

Pierce Edgecombe esq., sonne and heire of Richard Edgecombe kt. holdeth freely to him and his heires for ever in soccage' in Tregian 7 ac. C., fine 1s 2d, rent 18s 6½d.

	Fine	Rent
id. 12 ac. C.	1s	37s 7d
John Arundell of Trerise: quarter of 4 ac. C. in Landraith [St Blazey] and Pengelly	1s	37s 7d
John Killiow esq.: the same	1s	37s 7d
Oliver Saule esq., s. and heir of Nicholas Saule: the same		
Thomas Cole esq.: the same	1s	8s 7d
	in all	in all
Heirs of the Earl of Devon: 2 ac. C. in Trewerrin	1s 4d	9s 9¾d
Charles Trevannion kt.: 2 ac. C. in Trewerrin	1s 4d	9s 9¾d
William Carlyon: 1 ac. C. in Mevegwese and Meneginnis [Menagwins]	3d	2s 4d
David Hicks alias Trewargam: ½ ac. C. in Boskoweneth formerly John Boskoven's	2d	1s 9½d
Ezechiell Arundell esq. and Oliver Saule esq.: ½ ac. C. in Austell [St Austell]	2d	11¾d
Oliver Saule: moiety of ½ ac. C. in Carnaughte; William Crufte: the other moiety	2d	2s 0¾d
John Trelowan in the right of Jenefride his w., widow of John Stoddon: ½ ac. C. in Boskanny alias Boskavy [Biscovey], previously Robert and Phillip Wosas	2d	1s 4d
Edward Hearle esq.: ½ farl. in Boskanny [? Biscovey], previously Robert Martin's	0¾d	6d
Robert Hawkin: moiety of ½ farl. C. in Boskanny: Thomas Killiow esq.: the other moiety; previously Richard Trenowosicke's	0¾d	6d
William Hambly gent.: a farl. in Duporthe [Duporth], previously John Trewilliams	1d	1s
Olive Saule esq.: ½ ac. C. in Castle-gothowe [Castlegotha], previously		

	Fine	Rent
John Castlegothowes; pays at Michaelmas only	2d	1s 11¾d
id.: ½ ac. C. in Castlegothowe	2d	1s 11¾d
id.: ten. and 1 ac. C. in Boskawey [Boskavy], previously John Boskenweys	2d	1s 4d
Charles Durte gent.: ten. in Polreden and 1 ac. C.	suit of court only	
Oliver Saule kt., by death of Nicholas S. esq.: 2 ac. C. in Penrise [Penrice], previously Reginald de Penreis	nil	10s 2¼d
John Clowberry esq., by death of Oliver C. gent.: 4 ac. C. in Trewidell [Trewhiddle], previously Nicholas Trewidell's	2s	7s 6d
Richard Moyle gent.: 1½ ac. C. in Trevesecke [Trevissick]	6d	5s 6d
John Colquite gent.: 1 farl. in St Austell	1d	6d
Richard Moyle gent., by death of William Williams: 1 farl. in St Austell	1d	6d
Peter Courtney esq., by death of George C. gent.: ½ ac. C. in Carwarth [Carvarth]	2d	2s 0¾d
Humphrey Noye esq., by death of Edward N. esq.: two-thirds of a moiety of 1 farl. in Carwarth; John Mineheere: the other third; Oliver Saule esq.: the other moiety	1d	1s 0¼d and half ¼d
Humphrey Noye, as above: 1 farl. in Carwarth	1d	1s 0¼d and half ¼d
Edward Coisgarden: 1½ ac. C. in Trevarrecke	9d	5s 1½d
Thomas Lowre esq., s. and heir of William L. kt.: ½ ac. C. in Treverdecke [Treverdicke in margin]	3d	1s 7½d
Thomas Cole: moiety of ½ ac. C. in Boscavey; Jonathan Rashleigh esq., by death of John R.: the other moiety	2d	1s 4d
John Killiow jn. esq.: 1 ac. and 1½ farl. in Boscavey	7½d	4s 11½d
The heirs of Killiow, namely Natheniell Thorne in right of his w., and [—] Hodge, in right of his w.: ½ and ¼ farl. in Boscavey	0¾d	6d
John Lord Roberts, by death of Richard Lord Roberts: 1½ farl. in Boscavey	2d	1s
Richard White and Richard Dadow: 1 farl. in Boskennavighan	2d	1s 9d

	Fine	Rent
John Killiow of Lansallos jn. gent.: moiety of ½ ac. C. in Porth [Par]; Peter Laa: the other moiety	2d	1s
Charles Trubody: 3 farl. in Boscowall	3d	2s 8d
John Lord Roberts: one 'bedam' Mill [*see* p. vi] in Pentewan [*id.*]	nil	6d
Charles Trubody gent.: 9 parts of 13 parts of 1 ac. C. in Bosconwall [Boscundle]; John Clowberry esq.: $\frac{1}{13}$; Jenefride Stodden, by the death of John S.:$\frac{1}{13}$; William Hambley gent.: $\frac{1}{13}$; John Hodge gent.: the residue	1s	9s 10¾d
Total rents of assize	£8 13s	3½d + ¼d

'CONVENTIONARY TENNANTS OF INHERITANCE

Oliver Saule esq., by death of Mary Saule widow, holdeth in free conventionary to him and his heirs for ever from seven yeares to seven yeares a messuage in Towyn [Towan], fine 9s, rent 8s.

	Fine	Rent
id.: mess. in Towyn	6s	8s
John Oppie, in his own right: moiety of mess. in Towyn; Richard Opye, by surrender of John Opie: the other moiety	9s	8s
Oliver Saule: mess. in Towyn	9s	8s
id.: piece called Chappell land in Towyn	2s	1s
id.: mess. in Towyn, previously Thomas Whettres	3s	8s
id.: mess. in Towyn	4s 6d	4s
id.: 3 parts of 5 parts of a pasture called Fentengellan, and ⅕ of the same; John Opie: the other fifth	2s	1s
id.: moiety of mess. in Fentengellan; John Opie: ¼; Richard Opie, by surr. of John O.: ¼ mess.	9s	8s
id.: mess. in Towyn	4s 6d	4s
id.: mess. in Towyn	9s	8s
Alice Dadow, wid. of John D.: mess. and certain lands in Trenoweth [Trenowa]	3s 4d	9s
id.: mess. in Trenoweth, previously Edward Lawrence	3s 4d	3s
id.: mess. in Trenoweth, previously Edward Lawrence	3s 4d	10s
id.: mess. in Trenoweth, previously Edward Lawrence	2s	3s 6d

John Rowse, by surr. of Peter Rowse: 22 parts of
mess. and 12 ac. in ½ ac. C. divided into 42
parts in Nansmelyn; John Bennett by d. of

	Fine	Rent
Philip B. and Symon Bonny, by surr. of John Kiliowe: the residue, namely 20 parts	3s 4d	11s
id.: mess. and 11 ac. in ½ ac. C. in Nansmelyn	5s	11s
id.: mess. and 11 ac. in ½ ac. C. in Nansmelyn	5s	11s
id.: mess. and 11 ac. in ½ ac. C. in Nansmelyn	5s	9s
Peter Laa: mess and 7 ac. in Marthyn [Merthen] late William Laa	6s 8d	7s 6d
id.: mess. and 7 ac. in Marthyn, [late William L.][1]	6s 8d	7s 6d
Edmond Michell in right of Joan his w., late w. of Jeromie Foslett: mess. in Duporthe 'for seven yeares if his wife shall soe long live, which after the death of his said wife is to fall to the next heire of the said Jeromie Foslett'.	8s 6d	9s
Oliver Saule, by death of Nicholas S. his f.: mess. and 7 ac. in Castlegothowe	10s	7s 1½d
Samuel Hext, by surr. of John Hodge and Constance his w.: moiety of mess. and 5 ac. in Trenyaren [Trenarren] except a piece of land of about ¼ ac. and $\frac{1}{10}$ of the common within 'the Bulworkes of the Greate Quarry unto the hedges of Leslannow; John Melyn in right of his w., late w. of Nicholas Burnard, by the surr. of Oliver Burnard, holds this piece; John Denis, by surr. of William Goble: the $\frac{1}{10}$ of the common; Nicholas Cradocke, by death of Elizabeth C. wid: the other moiety except 10 perches; Daniel Bond, by surr. of Nicholas Cradocke: 6 perches; Andrew Cradocke, by the same surr.: the other 4 perches	9s	11s
Samuel Hext, by the same surr: moiety of a tenure in Trenyaren; Tristram Carlyon, by surr. of Richard Cradocke: the other moiety except 2 ac. lying 'in or neere the Cliffes conteyning the tenth parte of the Cliffes. David Moyle gent.: the said 2 ac. 'except the right of the lord of the Mannor to and in all quarries and royalties in the said tenth parte'	2s	3s
John Pearce, by the death of Michell P. his f.: moiety of ten. in Trenyaron; Samuel Hext, by surr. of John Hodge and Constance his w.: the other moiety	8s	7s 8d
id.: by the same death: moiety of another ten. there; Samuel Hext, by same surr.: the other moiety, except 5 ac. 'in the seate of Trenyaron'. Oliver Saule esq., by death of Mary Saule wid.: the said 5 ac.	2s	8s 4d

[1] In PRO text only.

	Fine	Rent
William Bond, by death of Johan B. his m.: 2 ten. with 10 ac. in Trenyaren, 'except one seller, two houses and one garden'. Daniell Bond, by surr. of William B. his f.: the said cellar. Mathew B., by the same surr.: one of the houses; Hugh Oliver: the other house and garden	10s	7s 6d
Luke Clements, by death of Anne his m.: moiety of 2 mess. and 10 ac. in Trenyaren; John Carlyon, by surr. of Amy Gitchard and Walter Morris her hbd.: the other moiety, except the right of common 'in the Cliffes from the Gerrand [Gerrans Point] to Gwindred [Gwendra Point].' David Moyle gent., by surr. of Richard M. his f.: the said right of common	10s	6s 6d
id.: as above: moiety of mess. and 5 ac. and ⅓ of a mess. and 5 ac. in Trenyaren; John Carlyon, by surr. of Amy Gitchard and Walter Morris: the other moiety, except right of common in the cliffs; David Moyle gent., by the same surr: common in the cliffs	8s	8s 8d
Mathew Bond, by surr. of William B. his f.: piece of land of 25 perches, being $\frac{5}{50}$ of a ten. in Trenyaren; Tristram Carlyon, in his own right: close called the Higher Tretheage alias Carveage of 2¼ ac. and 5 perches, being a fifth of the said ten.; William Hambley gent. in his own right: 2 ac. near the cliffs containing $\frac{1}{10}$ of the cliffs 'between the Greate Quarry and Leslannow', being $\frac{1}{25}$ of the said ten., except the right of the lord of the manor to all quarries and royalties; Tristram Carlyon, by surr. of Luke Evans: close called the Gew Parke and the stich in Pendrenicke being a $\frac{1}{17}$ part. The said Tristram, by surr. of Mathew Evans: moiety of the said ten. except 2 closes, a house and garden with a way to the garden and a rickplace. Elizabeth Evans, by the death of Mathew her hbd: said 2 closes, house, garden and way	8s	8s 8d
Marke Higman, by surr. of Walter H. and Elizabeth his w.: mess. and 5 ac. in ½ farl. in Trevisecke	11s 2½d	5s
William Gitchard, by surr. of John G. his bro.: mess. and 5 ac. in ½ ac. [sic] C. in Trevisecke	9s	5s
Oliver Saule esq., by death of John S. his bro.: mess. and 8 ac. in Penventon, late John Penwens	4s	8s
John Lillicke, in right of Alice his w.: moiety of mess. in Penventon Robin, lately William		

	Fine	Rent
Johns, except a close; Mathew Bond, by surr. of William John: the said close; Henry Carlyon gent., by surr. of William John: the other moiety	6s 8d	12s
id.: moiety of mess. and 3 ac.; Henry Carlyon by same surr.: the other moiety	6s 8d	1s 6d
Francis Scobell, by death of Richard S. his f.: 3 parts of a mess. in Penventon Searle; David Moyle gent., by surr. of Richard M.: ¼ part	2s	10s
id.: 3 parcels in Nansennes containing 15 ac.	6s 8d	1s
John Davies, by death of John D. his f.: mess. and 6 ac. in Polglasse [Polglase]	8s	7s
id.: as above: mess. and 6 ac. in Polglasse	3s 6d	3s 6d
id. as above: 2 ac. in Polglasse	5s 8d	6s 8d
David Moyle gent., by surr. of Richard M. his f.: 2 mess. and 13 ac. in Pencarrowe	10s	10s
Margarett Julyan wid., by death of Richard J. her hbd: mess. in Pencarrowe and 26 ac.	10s	10s
Walter Higman, by death of William H. his f.: 4 mess. and 26 ac. in Porthtowan [*id.*]	10s	18s
David Moyle gent., by death of Richard M. his f.: mess. and 3 ac. in Bohampton	12s	3s
id.: 6 ac. in Bohampton	12s	3s
[—] Clobury, by death of Oliver C. gent.: 2 mess. in Hea	10s	12s
Oliver Saule esq.: a corn mill with suit of mulcture of all the tenants of the manor, except the residents in the town of St Austell	2s	12s
[—] Lower, by death of Thomas L. esq.: 'suite of muleture of all the tennants of the mannor within the towne of St Austell'	1s 8d	1s 8d
Oliver Saule esq., by the death of John S. his bro.: ten. in St Austell	nil	2s
Walter Higman, by death of William H. his f.: 'one quarry of stone called freestone Quarry'	nil	1s 4d
Oliver Saule, by death of his bro.: 'quarry called Hellingstone Quarry'	nil	6s 8d

Peter Rickard, by surr. of Oliver Julian: mess. and 5 ac. in Trenyaren, except a close of 2 ac. and the right of common in the cliffs thereto belonging; also moiety of another mess. and 5 ac., except 3 houses, 2 gardens and rick-place, and the right of common belonging to the said ten. Marke Higman, by surr. of Oliver Julyan: the said close. Oliver Saule, by surr. of Oliver Julyan: right of common in the cliffs; Mathew Higman and William Harris: 2 houses and a garden; John Higman,

	Fine	Rent
by surr. of Peter Rickard: the other house and garden with the rick place	2s	7s 8d
William Pierce, by death of Richard P. his f.: mess. and 7 ac. in Trenyaren	8s	8s
'The tennants of this Mannor doe give in way of acknowledgement to the lord . . . for the lands and tenements . . . the some of forty shillings to be paid within six yeares after every assession' worth p.a.[2]		6s 8d
Oliver Saule esq., by death of John S. his bro.: mess. and 6 ac. in Penventon Lawrey	3s	10s
id.: 2 mess. and 5 ac. in Penventon Lawrey	9s	3s 4d
'All the parish of St Austell hold the assize of bread and ale within the said parish with stalledge for all the tennants there for which they pay for all services whatsoever' p.a.		2s
Oliver Saule, by death of John his Bro.: mess. and 7 ac. in Castlegotha	7s 1½d	7s 1½d
id.: by death of Nicholas Saule: mess. and 7 ac. in Castlegotha	nil	7s 1½d
id.: by death of Marie S. wid.: close called Blackheade [Black Head, near Trenarren] of 5 ac. 'lying neare the seaside and was separated from out of the tenements of Trenyaren'	6s	2s

'Severall parcells of pastures and quarries hereafter menconed are held by the present tennants untill the next assessions onely'. David Moyle, in the name of all the tenants of Tewington: moiety of the pasture of Gwallon, Portmellyn and Towyn, in all 360 ac.; John Stephens in the name of all the tenants of St Austell and Carverth: the other moiety, except the right of the lord to all encroachments and buildings newly erected upon the said grounds without licence of the lord; and also the right of all the tenants of Tewington therein, for which they pay the rent of 33s 4d. Impr. val. £18.[3]

Oliver Saule and Francis Scoble: certain parcels of waste 'neare the seaside betweene Garren and Gwindrith, together with a wharfe or key thereon built at theire owne chardges for the keepeing of nets and other services, together with a roweable way for all manner of cariadges until the next assessions onely' Rent 2s yearly and 'alsoe repaireing and susteyning the said Wharfe or key at theire owne costs and expences'. Impr. Val. 18s.

Oliver Saule esq. and David Moyle gent.: a piece of land called Polkeare until the next assessions. Rent 5s. Impr. val. 15s.

---

[2] This as was noted in the margin, was Old Knowledge Money.
[3] The membrane is endorsed (15 October 1652) to the effect that the right of the tenants to the common of Gwallon Down has been sustained. Its area put at 380 acres.

Francis Scobell, until next assessions: 'quarry of stone in Treniaren extend-
ing from a quarry called Higman Quarry unto Roopehaven [Ropehaven] to
and in the Greate Quarry, with liberty to erect and build houses and
buildings in and upon the premises' Rent 20s. Impr. val. £6.

John Hodge, till the next assession: piece of land in Gwallen 'neare the
seaside', 200 ft long and 30 ft broad, on which he has built a cellar, with
liberty of ingress, egress and regress. Fine, to be paid in 6 years after the last
assessions 6s 8d. Rent 3s 4d. Impr. val. 10s.

Oliver Saule: royalties of the manor. Fine 6d. Rent 1s.

Md. 'wee have certified the value of the Toll Tynn . . . in grosse with our
retorne of the lease thereof herewith sent up; and that the last Assessions
held for this Mannor were in the 11 September 1645.

Boundes of the said Mannor

This mannor is bounded on the west partly by a rocke called Scoonhoth and
partly by the parish of Mevagissey; on the north part by the Mannor of
Trenance Austell and partly with the Mannor of Treverbin Courtney; on
the east parte with a bridge called Blazye [St Blazey] Bridge, and a rocke
called Killiwarther [Killyvarder Rock], and on the south part by the sea.

Comons

Comons enioyed by the tennants . . . unstinted and claimed by them as part
of their customary tenements, the rents and fines for the same being
included in the rents and fines paid by the said customary tennants.'

Customs

An assessions court is held every seven years; a court leet twice yearly and a
court baron every three weeks. Tenants pay old and new recognition money.
Choice of reeve and his duties. Choice of tithingman and beadle and
'viewers of reparacons'.
Free tenants pay a relief and customary, a heriot.
If any encroachment is made on the lord's waste, or new houses built, those
concerned are to come to the Assession and 'take the same at the lord's hand
under such rent and for such tyme as shall please the lord', or the lord may
take it for his own use.

An Abstract of the Present Rents, Future Improvements and other Profits of the Manor

Rents of assize and perquisites of court	£15 3s 3¾d
Rents of conventionary tenants	£23 17s 2¼d
Fines and Old Knowledge money	£3 2s 2½d
	and seventh of 6 farthings
Woods are worth beside the rent	£2 3s 4d
New Knowledge money	£1 10s
Total	£45 16s 0¾d
	and seventh of 6 farthings
Improved value of conventionary lands	£26 3s
Woodland now worth	£8

'This is an Exact Survey . . . [Sd]'

42   MANOR OF TIBESTA

DCO S/5; PRO E 317 (C)/44. This was an ancient manor of the Duchy, occupying very approximately the parish of Creed.

'A Survey of the Mannor of Tibesta . . . retorned [3 April 1650].

There are within the said mannor two parcells of woodground, the one called Coiseclise, the other Girlinnicke [Carlenick] wood, the fallinge of which woods doe belong to the Lord . . . But the herbage and under weedeings thereof is claymed by the tennants of Coiseclise and Girlinnicke as parte of their tenements. The said woodgroundes conteyne by mensuracon' 40 ac. and are worth p.a. £8.
'The wood now groweing . . . of about twenty yeares groweth' is worth £200.

'FREETENNANTS OF THE SAID MANNOR

John Carew esq., holdeth freely to him and his heires for ever in soccage eight acres and a halfe of land Cornish in Bosewengam, Trindan, Trewidan alias Trewidane, Heligin [Heligan in St Ewe], Pensagolus [Pensagillas in St Ewe] and Regian [Tregian in St Ewe]' paying, at Christide 18d, at Easter, 4s 7d, at Midsomer 18d and at Michaeltide, 4s 6¼d, in all 12s 1¼d.
Pierce Edgecombe esq., s. and h. of Richard E.; 1 ac. in Trewolgham, paid as above, 3s10d;[1]   *id.*: 3 ac. in Tregriggowa [Tregidgeo], Treisin, Fentenwin [Ventontinny] and Penkes Mill, previously Henry of Bandrighams, paid as above, 6s 9d;   *id.*: 1½ ac. C. in Lake and Tencracke [Trencreek], as above, 3s 10d;   Thomas Hawke, moiety of 1 ac. C. in Carwinnecke [Carwinnick];   Thomas Mineheire, the other moiety, 3s 8d. Aid money 6d.
Nathaniell Mohun gent., 4 parts in 9 of 1 ac. C. in Trencreake, and 2 parts of 1 ac. C. in Trenwallecke [Trevillick]; Robert and John Polewheele esq., the residue, 2s 6d;   Thomas Hawke, 1 farl. in Carwinnecke, 2s;   *id.*: 1 ac. C. in Carwinnecke, 4s 2d;   Nathaniell Mohun gent., 4 parts in 9 of 1 ac. C. in Trencreake;   Robert Penwarne, 4 parts, and John Polewheele the rest 12d;   John Tanner esq., one course of water running to the mill of Nanslason alias Nanlenson 4d;   *id.*, moiety of 3 parts in 10 parts divided of another moiety of 1 ac. C. in Bosullian [Bossillian]; John Strangewayes kt., $\frac{1}{10}$ of a moiety; John Windham kt., $\frac{1}{10}$; the heirs of Marten, $\frac{1}{10}$; John Tanner, by the death of Bevile his gdf., $\frac{1}{10}$; John Coke esq., by death of John C. his f., $\frac{1}{10}$; the heirs of Leigh, the other $\frac{1}{10}$, 3s.
id., moiety of 3 parts in 10 parts of another moiety of lands formerly Roger Keizzell in Nanlassen [Nanclassen] and Tregamarras and 3 ac. C.; John Strangewayes kt., $\frac{1}{10}$ of the said moiety; John Windham kt., $\frac{1}{10}$; heirs of Marten, $\frac{1}{10}$; John Tanner, $\frac{1}{10}$; John Hornewood, $\frac{1}{10}$; John Coke, $\frac{1}{10}$; heirs of Leigh, $\frac{1}{10}$, suit of court only; Elizabeth Grosse, by the death of Charles G. her f., 'one beda mill with a course of water', 4d;   John Arundell of Lanherne kt., 1 ac. C. in Rosekada, 4s 4½d;   Nicholas Biscowen esq., by death of Hugh B., 1 ac. C. in Trewarvena [Trewarmenna] 1s 1d;   Nicholas Boscawen: 1 ac. C. in Trewelveswortha [Trevilvas in Probus] 3s 6d. Aid money 6d.

---

[1] The rent of this and next two tenements were payable quarterly and in unequal amounts.

Richard Blake, 3 farl. in Reskada, 2s 6d;   Edward Herle esq.,$\frac{1}{3}$ of certain land in Rozerrye alias Zerriggaie; Hugh Williams gent.:$\frac{1}{3}$ of land called Trestrainwolas, and Francis Wills esq. likewise, another third called Trestrailewarth, the whole being 3 ac. C. in Trestraile and Rosfrighe alias Rosewerry, 5s 6d;   William Corriton, 2 ac. C. in Honyslo alias Honyshall and Fentenkenin [Ventontinny] 4s 6d; Elizabeth Grosse by the death of Charles G. her f., 1 ac. C. in Bosulian Volas, 3s 6d;   John Trefrie esq., by the death of Ursula T., 3 farl. and $\frac{1}{3}$ of an ac. C. in Roskada, 2s 6d; John Trefusis esq. and Francis Godolphin de Treveneage, 1 ac. C. in Polkehigon 2s, and for stable, 5$\frac{1}{2}$d, 2s 5$\frac{1}{2}$d;   John Lord Roberts, by the death of Richard Lord Roberts, 3 ac. C. in Girgoes [Gargus], Tresengowan [Tregonjohn] and Tregensith 9s 6d.

Total   £4 2s 11$\frac{1}{4}$d

'CONVENTIONARY TENNANTS OF THE SAID MANNOR

Benedict Perdue holdeth in free conventionary to him and his heires for ever from seven yeares to seven yeares one messuage and [19 ac.] of land English in halfe an acre of land Cornish in Tibestammeere [Tibesta] for which he payeth' p.a. 9s and fine, 11s 2d.

	Rent	Fine
id., mess. and 20 ac. in $\frac{1}{2}$ ac. C. in Tibestameere	9s	11s 8d
William Wolridge: mess. and 19 ac. in $\frac{1}{2}$ ac. C. in Tibestameere	9s	6s
Md. the said William W. is to keep the houses in repair, 'to drain the marrish ground belonginge thereto, to till or eare up according to the quantity of the said tenement upon pain of forfeiture'		
Arthur Evans, by surr. of Benedict Purdue: mess. and 16 ac. in $\frac{1}{2}$ ac. C. in Tibesta Werring	8s	24s
Michael Treghue, by the death of Bernard Tanner esq.: moiety of a mess., being 16 ac. in $\frac{1}{2}$ ac. C. in Trevaleicke [Trevillick]	7s	3s
id., moiety of a mess. being 20 ac. in $\frac{1}{2}$ ac. C. in Trevalecke [Trevillick]	5s	3s
id., mess. and 21 ac. in $\frac{1}{2}$ ac. C. in Trevalecke	10s	14s 8d
id., mess. in Trevallecke and 21 ac. in $\frac{1}{2}$ ac. C.	10s	21s
id., piece of waste ground in Presthineck [Presthillick]	1s 3d	nil
Md. M. T. 'is admitted taker of the severall tenements and takings aforesaid in trust onely and for the benefitt of Hugh Boscawen gent., Elizabeth his wife and theire children for the performance of articles of agreement formerly entered into by Bernard Tanner esq., of the one part and the said Hugh Boscawen and Elizabeth of the other parte' dated 1 May 1625.		
Joan Lawrence wid., by death of John L. her hbd: 2 mess. and 18 ac. in Nantellan [Nantellan]	9s	10s
id., mess. and 18 ac. part of 5 farl., and 2 ac. of waste in Nantellan	9s	3s 4d

	Rent	Fine
id., mess. and 18 ac. in ½ ac. C. in Nantellan	9s	6s
id., 2 ac. waste near Coislane in Nantellan	1s	nil
Henry Huddy, by surr. of John H. his f.: 5 mess. and 42 ac. in 3 farl. in Pennas [Penans]	25s	25s
Elenor Williams wid., by death of Richard W. her hbd., 56 ac. in Crugglas [Cruglaze]	1s	2s 6d
Peter Herle, by surr. of Dorothy Pardue sp., moiety of a piece of land in the borough of Grampont [Grampound] with a croft of land adjoining, 2 ac. of arable and 1 ac. of land in the Lord's commons	1s	2s 6d
Walter Hawkins, by surr. of Trewenard Kestle, ten. with a garden in Grampont	5s 9d	nil
Michael Treglyne, moiety of a piece of land within the borough of Grampont with a croft adjoining and 2 ac. of arable and 1 ac. in the Lord's commons	1s	2s 6d
M. Tregline: certain lands and tenements called Coveley, previously John Dyar of Grampont	4s	4s
John Woldridge,⅓ mess. and 58 ac. and 27 perches in Garlinnicke; Ralphe Woldridge the other two parts	11s 5d	15s 9½d
id., in his own right,⅓ of a mess. and 58½ ac. 27 perches and the third parte of a perch' in Garlinnicke; Ralphe W the other 2 parts of the mess. and land	11s 5d	15s 9½d
Jocosa Harrison wid., 6 ac. waste in a croft called Penrocke in the village of Garlinnicke	3s	1s

Md. 'Thomas Hoblin came at the last Assession and claimed a moiety of the said tenement or wast by right of a surrender by Rosa, sister of Jocosa. Upon the debate whereof there being noe president shewed nor proofe made before the Commissioners that the eldest daughter had ever enioyed alone any customary tenement in this manner after the death of her father from her other sisters.'

	Rent	Fine
Ralphe Wolridge, a close and a pinfold of the Lord's in Bagheykeyer	3s 4d	nil
Elenor Williams, by the death of Richard W. gent., her hbd., moiety of mess. and 12 ac. in⅓ ac. C. in Luscoyes	6s	6s 8d
id., the other moiety of the same	3s	3s 4d
id., moiety of another mess. in Luscoyes and 13 ac. and 3 parts of an ac. C.	6s	8s
id., the other moiety of the same	3s	6s 8d
John Polkinhorne: moiety and ¾ of the other moiety of a mess. and 25 ac. in Trekine [Trecaine]; Thomas Hawke ¼ of the said moiety	8s	28s 4d

	Rent	Fine
id., moiety and ¾ of the other moiety of another mess. in Trekine and 17 ac. 2½ perches in ½ ac. C.; Thomas Hawke the other ¼	5s 4d	15s 4d
id., moiety and ¾ of the other moiety of a mess. in Trekine and 25 ac. in ½ ac. C.; Thomas Hawke, the other ¼	8s	26s 8d
id., moiety and ¾ of the other moiety of a mess. and 8 ac. in⅓ of halfe an ac. C.; Thomas Hawke the other ¼	8s	13s 4d
Reginald Soccombe, 7 mess. and 38 ac. and 3 perches in Trewinowinre [Trewinnow-meor]	17s	23s 4d
Edward Blighe, in right of Julian his w., ⅓ mess. and 28 ac. in 1 ac. C. in Trewinowinre; James Hughes other ⅔	8s	3s 4d
id., ⅓ mess. and 18 ac. in ½ ac. C. in Trewinowinre; James Hughe the other⅓	8s	3s 4d
id., ⅓ mess and 18½ ac. in ½ ac. C. in Trewinowinre; James Hughe the other⅔	8s	3s 4d
Henry Huddy, by surr. of John H.: mess. and 20 ac. in ½ ac. C. in Treswallen [Treswallen]	9s	4s
id., mess. and 19 ac. in ½ ac. C. in Treswallen	9s	4s
Mathew Andrew, ¾ of a moiety of a mess. and 18 ac. in ½ ac. C. in Trevelvaswolas [Trevilvas]; John Buddle, 3 parts of ¼; Peter Corriew [Carew], ¼ of a ¼; Reskiner Courteney, ¼ of the other moiety and moiety of another ¼; Joan Marrett wid., 7 parts of 8 parts of the moiety of the said ¼; Anthony Slade, the said ⅛ of the moiety of a quarter	8s	7s 6d
id., ¾ of a moiety of a mess. and 18 ac. in ½ ac. C. in Trevelvaswolas; John Buddle, ¾ of a ¼ of a moiety; Peter Cornew, ¼ of a ¼; Reskiner Courtney, ¼ of the other moiety, and moiety of a ¼; Joan Marrett wid., 7 parts of 8 parts of a moiety of the said ¼; Anthony Slade, ⅛ of said quarter	4s 6d	2s 6d
The same persons: the same fractions of a mess. and 18 ac. in ½ ac. C. in Trevelvaswolas	4s 6d	3s 4d
The same persons hold similar fractions of mess. and 18 ac.	8s	3s 4d
John Pearce, by marr. of Jane P. his m., mess. and 36 ac. in 1 ac. C. in Carevosa [Carvossa in Probus]	16s	40s
id., mess. and 18 ac. in ½ ac. C. in Carewosa	9s	nil
Benedict Pardue., mess. and 18 ac. in ½ ac. C. in Casobie (Casoby)	9s	8s
William Williams: a moiety, and John Hearle, the other moiety of 2 mess. and 38 ac. in Broughteliver [Barteliver], rent 13s 4d; also of another mess. and 38 ac. at a rent of 13s 4d, and of a		

	Rent	Fine
piece of land called Croft of 2 ac. at a rent of 10d and a piece called the Quarrie at a rent of 6d.	28s	28s
Walter Quarme clerk, mess. and 3 parts of a mess. and 53 ac. and 27 perches in 3 farl. in Nanscroffwolas [Nancor] at a rent of 18s.; another mess. and 17½ ac. in 1¼ farl. at a rent of 7s.	25s	25s
Richard Huddy, by surr. of John H. his f., 2 mess. and 17 ac. in 1 farl. in Carnere alias Carvere	6s	6s
Walter Quarme: mess. and 20 ac. in ½ ac. C. in Nanscrowfwartha	9s	3s 4d
id., mess. and 21 ac. in ½ ac. C. in Nanscrofwartha	11s	nil
Henry Huddy, by surr. of John H. his f. mess. and 31 ac. in 1 farl. in Pengelley [Pengelley]	13s 4d	20s
Elenor Williams wid., by death of Richard W. her hbd.: certain lands in Coisterne of 80 ac.; previously Nicholas Otes who paid 9s rent. Now E. W. pays	20s	nil
John Pearce, by marr. of Johan P. wid. his m.: mess. and 23 ac. in ½ ac. C. in Fentenscowell	8s	8s
Jocosa Herrison wid., in her own right (excepting the right of Rosa her sister), 10 ac. and⅓ ac., previously Ralphe Cooke's; 10 ac. and⅓ ac. in 1 farl., previously John Marke's, and 2 mess. previously Thomas Seya, with 19 ac. in Trewinnowe	17s 6d	9s 8d
John Tredinham gent., piece of land called Cregotrewarthan [Crego] of ½ ac.		
Charles Trevanion kt., for 7 years, the fishing, hunting, fowling and taking of birds within the Manor	1s	6d
The Bailiff of the Hundred of Powder pays the lord of this manor p.a.	40s	
The Bailiff of the Manor of Tywarnayle pays	6s 8d	

'BOUNDES OF THE MANNOR[2]

This Mannor is bounded on the east with the parish of St Ewe alias Eva, on the south with parts of the foresaid parish and the parish of Cuby, the lands of Hugh Boscawen, William Corriton and the heires of Ezekiell Grosse esq., on the west with the lands of Richard Williams gent. called Swarne Fields and the lands of Sir John Arundell kt, and alsoe with the lands of Edward Herle esq. called Tregoofe and on the north with the lands of Pierce Edgecombe, John Vivian and Hugh Boscawen esq., and with the parish of St Stephens in Brannell and the lands of John Tanner and Edward Herle esq.'.

Md. 'that there lyeth within the boundes of this Mannor the Borroughe of Grampont heretofore parte of the said Mannor, but by John Earle of

[2] A reconstruction of this manor by Charles Henderson is included in the Henderson *Calendar*, II, 369, Royal Institution of Cornwall, Truro.

Cornewall and afterwards King of England it was made a free borroughe by his charter, wherein there is graunted unto the burgesses thereof divers priviledges with the rents of the said borroughe . . . in fee farme for ever by the yearely rent of £12 11s 4d.

'Comons belonging to the said Mannor

There are certeine comons . . . in which all the tennants claime right of pasture unstinted and have accordingly enioyed the same time out of minde. The said comons are knowen by the name of Talfrew Comons'.

Customs of the Manor

Two courts leet are held each year, and a court baron every three weeks. A reeve is chosen at one of them.

Free tenants owe a relief oon each death or alienation; customary tenants owe a heriot.

An Assessions court is held every seven years; New Knowledge money is paid.

Widows may continue to hold their husbands' tenements during their widowhood.

No customary tenant may surrender his estate out of the manorial court 'except the Steward be sicke and cannott come or that he doth willfully absent himselfe. And if soe, that the the tithingman and reeve (being first desired) ought to come with two other of the tennants either to the tennants house being within the Mannor or unto any other parte of the Mannor. And there the partie desireing to surrender (being in perfect memory) may make a surrender to whom he pleaseth. And the said reeve and tithingman are to present the same unto the steward or his sufficient deputy at the nexte courte followinge such surrender (who is to take the same for a lawful surrender and receiveing six pence for his fees, is to enter the said surrender into the Courte rolles according to the custome'.

An Abstract of the present Rents and other Profits of the said Manor

Rents of assize and perquisites	£7 12s 7d
Auxilliary or aid money	1s
Rents of conventionary tenants	£26 14s 5d
Fines, on average	£3 12s 9½d
Recognition money, on average	£1 10s
Value of woodland, per annum	£8
Total	£47 10s9½d
Wood now growing is worth	£200

'This is an exact survey . . . [sd]

43   MANOR OF TINTAGEL

DCO S/5; PRO E 317 (C)/45. This was an ancient manor of the Duchy. It occupied the greater part of the parish of Tintagel.

'A Survey of the Mannor of Tintagell . . . retorned [12 July 1650].

The Mannor or Mansion house comonly knowen by the name of King Arthur Castle alias Tintagell Castle.
The said castle is totally out of repair and much ruined, the materialls not beinge worth takeinge downe, the scite whereof as it now standeth conteynes aboute halfe an acre of land.'
Lands belonging to the said castle
King Arthurs Island: 'All that parcell of pasture ground knowen by the name of King Arthurs Island, conteyning by estimacion thirty acres; all those severall parcells of meadow ground in three severall peeces called Bossin Meade, Halmere and Dingle Downe alias Dingle Hey with the appurtenances' [11 ac., worth at an impr. val. p.a. £13].
Md. 'that John Billing of St Tuddy alias Udy [St Tudy] esq. hath now the possession . . . which he claimeth to hold by custome of the Mannor, the same being at first graunted to his father, but before that tyme it was held by John Arundell of Lanherne kt by letters patents; therefore wee conceave the same not customarie. the tennants of the said Mannor not owneing it to be customarie tenement. Neither had the commissioners appointed by the Dukes of Cornewall to keepe assessionarie courtes power to lett or alienate any thing from the Dukedom but for the terme of seven yeares and noe longer. The rent which the said Billing now paieth for the said Castle and Island is [6s 8d] and for the foresaid meadow the some of [36s 2d, together 42s 10d] which is answered at the auditt by the Reeve of the Mannor yearly.

Free-Tennants of the said Mannor

William Hender holdeth to him and his heires for ever in soccage halfe an acre of land Cornish in Hender for which he paieth' 1½d
Walter Batten gent., 1½ ac. C. in Tregartha [Tregatta] and Melidum Bell alias Menedewe, 5s 3½d;   Simon Foote, s. and h. of Lawrence F., ½ ac. C. in Menadon alias Menedew or 40 ac. English, 1s 5d.
Thomas Harvey, in right of Jane his w., [—] Kinge,[1] in right of Jacies his w., Thomas Day, in right of Katherin his w., and Thomas Mill, in right of Honor his w., daughters and heires of Roger Flamancke esq., ½ ac. C. in Tremron alias Trenire and Turvarth, 1s;   John Pearce, 1 ac. C. in Hendre in the parish of St David [Davidstow] 4s; The Reeve of Tintagel, a 'Bede' mill[2] of Hender Burnor [Hendraburnick in Davidstow] 1s; William Cotton cler., in right of his w., ten. in Bosiney Castle alias Botrian Castle [Bossiney, not Boscastle], 10d;   Nicholas Carlyon, 1 farl. C. in Tremrom alias Turwerth, 1s;   Anthony Nicholls esq., 3 ac. C. in Timpethie alias Tipethia [Penpethy in Tintagel] except 12 ac. E.; William Cotton cler., in right of his wife, the said 12 ac., 1s 3d;   Richard Rowe, moiety of ½ ac. C. in Menadew and Tregarth, Richard Curry the other moiety, 3s 5½d;   John Nicoll, by d. of John N. his f., 1 ac. C. in Menadew, 4s;   John Archer, 1 farl.

[1] This reading is uncertain. The name has been clumsily altered in both copies of the Survey.
[2] See p. vi.

in Tremron, 1s; The Colledge of Windsor, 2 closes called Trebesen in the parish of Tintagell, 1s; John Langford, lands called Langford Hele, 6d; John Woode esq., by d. of John W. his f., 35 ac. in Trewarman, [Trewarmett] by kt serv., no rent or suit of court.
John Lord Roberts, moiety of lands called Bestard alias Bastard [Bastard] in the parish of St Ginnis [St Gennys]; John Barron by the d. of John B. his uncle, the residue, two suits yearly to the lord's courts and 6d; Stephen Marshall, lands in the parish of St Ginnis called Treveege [Trevigue], 4d; Humphrey Lower, lands called Tremeere [Tremeer] in 'the parish of Udy alias Tudy [St Tudy]', 6d.

Total rents of assize   27s 2½d

CUSTOMARY TENANTS OF THE MANOR

Katherin Hemminge wid., by the d. of John H. her hbd., 'holdeth to her and her heires for ever and assignes in free conventionary from seven yeares to seven yeares . . . one messuage and [22 ac.] in Downrowe [Downrowe], except one close called West Towne and one meadow called Shutta Parke, conteyninge by estimacon [3 ac.] and John H. by the surrender of Henry Hemminge holdeth . . . the said two closes . . .', rent 10s, fine 18s.

	Rent	Fine
William Symons, moiety of a mess. and 20 ac. in Downrow; Pethericke Symons, the other moiety	10s	13s 4d
John Heyman, Clement Callaway, Richard Martin, mess. and 20 ac. in Downerowe	10s	2s 0½d
Katherine Hemminge wid., as above, curtelage and 9 ac. in 1 farl. C. in Hobbeland	3s 6d	4s
John Lord Roberts, by the d. of Lady Frances R. his m., mess. and 21 ac. in Halgeborne alias Halgerowe [Halgabron]	10s	15s
William Bray, Pentecost Symons and Richard Burneberry, mess. and 34 ac. in Halegeborne	10s	12s
Robert Tincke, by the d. of Joan T. his m., mess. and 43 ac. in Halgeborne	6s 8d	9s
Thomas Woode esq., by the d. of Sibella W. his m., 4 tenures and 16 ac. in Malskaffie, except the right of all the inhabitants of Tintagell 'for the use and sustentacion of the poore of the said place'	7s	6s 8d
John Browne, Nicholas B. and Anne B., mess. and 17 ac. in Venne	13s 4d	15s
John Symons, Jane S. and Nicholas Callowe, moiety of 2 mess. and 25 ac. in Trewise [Truas]	6s 2d	2s
Katherin Jory wid., the other moiety	12s	14s
John Symons, Jane S. and Nicholas Callow, mess. and 25 ac. in Trewise	12s	7s
John Lord Roberts, Jane Symons, Jerome Dangarte, Anne Bray and John Symons, mess. and 18 ac. in Fentanleigh [Fenterleigh]	9s	9s
John Symons, Lawrence Bray, Roger Ridgway, John Symons and Samuell Daw, mess. and 18 ac. in Fentenleigh	9s	5s

	Rent	Fine
Thomas Woode esq., Edith Philip and Samuell Daw, mess. and 18 ac. in Fentenleigh	9s	8s 6d
Thomas Woode, by the d. of Sibill W. his m., mess. and 18 ac. in Treneleigh alias Trewelleigh [Trevillett?]	8s	6s
id., as above, mess. and 18 ac. in Tremeleigh	8s	6s
id., mess. and 9 ac. in Tremeleigh	4s	3s 6d
id., mess. and 9 ac. in Tremeleigh	4s	3s 6d
Richard Davie, Anne Davie and Joan Panter, 2 mess. and 15 ac. in Trevellecke [Trevillick]	11s	12s
Christopher Worthyvale esq., 2 mess. and 16 ac. in Trevelleck	10s 6d	2s
Joan Stroute, mess. and 16 ac. and 1 ac. of meadow in Trengeiffe alias Trengeith	8s	6s
Lawrence Bray, Anne Cullow, Joan Stroute, mess. and 15 ac. in Trengeiffe	8s	6s
John Hemming, Katherin Jory, Thomas Dadgin, Samuell Daw and John Symons, mess. and 8 ac. in Trenhale [Trenale]	5s	6s
John Symons, moiety of mess. and 8 ac. in Trenhale; Margery Tincke, John Symons, Bartholomew Cornew and Thomas Padnor, the other moiety	5s	6s
id., moiety of mess. and 15 ac. in Trenhale; the others, as above, the other moiety	10s	13s
John Symons: the park of Bossiney	5s	nil
Stephen Robins, John Locke, William Symons, Robert Avery and Mathias Webb, mess. in Treworman [Trewarmett?]	10s	11s 6d
John Mellorne, John Locke, Nathaniell Pethicke, Isaac Broad, Penticost Symon, Thomas Mellorne, Jane Mellorne and William Millard, mess. in Treworman	10s	11s 6d
Theophilus Avery, William Murfield, Mathias Webb, Isaac Broade, William Millard, Thomas Woode esq., Edith Garland wid., Thomas Mellorne and Thomas Hoskin, mess. and 14 ac.	18s	12s
Isaac Broade, Mathias Webb and Robert Avery, mess. in Treworman	8s 2d	6s
John Hodge, Lawrence Bray, Thomas Mellorne, Margarett Parsons, Joseph Avery and Penticost Symons, 3 parts of a mess. and 18 ac. in Trenow [Treknow]	10s	9s
Mathew Sweetsen, Lawrence Bray, Mary Battin, and Jane Rush, Penticost Symon and Robert Avery, a mess. and a quarter of a mess. and 18 ac.	16s 8d	14s 9d
Thomas Mellorne, Thomas Woode esq., Mary Battin, Charles Niche, Joseph Avery and Joan Harper, mess. and 18 ac. in Trenow	13s 4d	11s
Margarett Parson, Henry Bray, Thomas Parson, John Arnold, Penticost Symons, mess. and 18 ac.	13s 4d	11s

	Rent	Fine
Penticost Symons, Clement Avery, Mary Batten, William Symons, moiety of a mess. and 26 ac. in Trenow; Robert Avery, the other moiety	26s 10d	22s
Richard Hayne, mess. and 16 ac. in Trewithan [Trewithen]	11s	10s 6d
John Parson and Alice P., mess. and 16 ac. in Trewithan	11s	10s 6d
id., mess. and 16 ac. in Trewithan	11s	10s 6d
Thomas Wills alias Hele and Joan W. wid., mess. and 40 ac. in Treseigh alias Bosleigh	11s	6s
id., mess. and 80 ac. there	11s	6s
Thomas Woode esq., a corn mill previously in the tenure of Lawrence Tincke and John Woode esq.	106s 8d	nil

Md. that Sibilla Woode wid. at the Assessions of 1626 claimed this mill 'but soe that she would pay but [23s 4d] rent which was not graunted to her by the court. Notwithstanding, Thomas Woode aforesaid refuseth to pay any more than the rent she then offered althoe the old rent be as aforesaid.'

	Rent	Fine
'All the tennants of the Mannor hold . . . the pasture of all that downe called Godelghon Downe [Condolden Down]' of 120 ac.	42s	nil
John Lord Roberts, by the d. of Frances his m., moiety 'of one rocke in the sea called Layrocke [Lye Rock]; John Locke, the other moiety	3d .	nil
Richard Haine, John Dungarte, Ralph Williams, Joan Stroute, 3 mess. and 24 ac. in Tregate [Tregatta]	21s	21s
Richard Haine, John Niche, Ralphe Williams, mess. and 8 ac. in Tregate	7s	7s
Katherin Jory, by the d. of Robert J. her hbd., mess. and 25 ac. in Trewis	6s 3d	4s
John Billing esq., by d. of Elizabeth B. his m., 'one rocke called the Sisters [The Sisters]'	8d	nil
Joan Stroute wid., 2 quarries in Landerdon	3s 4d	
Alice Parsons, 1 quarry	1s 8d	
Mathew Sweeteser, 1 quarry	1s 8d	
Nicholas Cullow, 1 quarry	1s 8d	
John Browne, Nicholas B. and Ann B., 2 quarries	2s 4d [sic][3]	
Thomas Woode esq. and John Nicle, 1 quarry	1s 8d	
Thomas Hoskin, 1 quarry	1s 8d	
John Symons, 1 quarry	1s 8d	
Katherin Hemminge, 1 quarry	1s 8d	
Henry Bray and Margarett Parson, 1 quarry	1s 8d	
The heirs of Moulsworthy, 4 quarries	6s 8d	

[3] Should be 3s 4d. This error occurs in both copies of the Survey.

	Rent	Fine
John Symons, 1 quarry	1s 8d	
Katherin Jory, 1 quarry	1s 8d	
[—] Danger, 1 quarry	1s 8d	
John Browne, 1 quarry	1s 8d	
Walter Tincke, 1 quarry	1s 8d	
Christopher Worthy Vale esq., royalty of fishing, hawking, hunting and catching birds until the next Assessions	1s	6s
Old knowledge money, on average	2s 2½d and ⅐ of 1d	

'THE BOUNDES OF THE SAID MANNOR

. . . on the west and north west with the sea; on the north with the vicaridge of the parish of Tintagell and the borroughe of Bossiney; on the north east with the parish of Trevalga; on the east with the lands of Mr Anthony Nicoll and Mr Glynn; on the south and south west with the Mannor of Trebarwith, being the lands of John Harrington esq.

CUSTOMS OF THE MANOR

An Assessions court is held every seven years; a court leet twice yearly, and a court baron every three weeks. At one of the meetings of the court leet a Reeve is chosen, who is to collect reliefs and perquisites worth 26s 8d.
Free tenants pay a relief and customary tenants, a heriot.
Widows may hold their late husbands tenement during their widowhood.
'For other customes of the said Mannor wee could not learne more, the jury for the said Mannor referringe us to the records of the Dukedome of Cornewall and the brests of auntient men of the said Mannor.'

AN ABSTRACT OF THE PRESENT RENTS AND FUTURE IMPROVEMENTS
OF THE SAID MANOR

Rents of assize and perquisites of court	£2 13s 10½d
Rents of conventionary tenants	£31 4s 4d
Fines of conventionary tenants, payable within six years after each Assession, on average	£2 15s10¾d and a⅐ part of ¼d
Old Knowledge money, on average	2s 2½d and a⅐ of ¼d
New knowledge money	10s
Rent of land let for seven years only	£2 2s 10d
	Total £39 9s 1¾d and a⅐ of ½d
Improved value of lands let in 1645 for seven years, besides the present rent, p.a.	£10 17s 2d

'This is an exact survey . . . [Sd].'

44 MANOR OF TINTEN

DCO S/5; PRO E 317 (C)46. The manor formed a compact area in the parish of St Tudy. It had formerly been held by Henry Courtenay, Marquis of Exeter, and was added to the Duchy in 1540.

'A Survey of the Mannor of Tinten . . . retorned [4 July 1650]

The Mannor or Mansion house knowen and called by the name of the Barton house of Tinten.
The said house consisteth of one faire hall, a kitchen and a larder below staires; above staires foure lodging chambers and a little roome adioyning; a little house open to the roofe for the keepeing of beere; one stable and an oxehouse.
The scite consisteth of one corte, an outyarde with a garden and two orchards conteyning two acres and a halfe.

DEMEASNES LAND LETT IN LEASE WITH THE FORESAID HOUSE
All that parcell of meadowe ground knowen by the name of the Little Broome Parke, conteyninge two acres'
Pasture, being 2 parts of a close called Broome Parke, 3ac.;   Pasture, 3 parts of 4 of Furse Parke, 3 ac.;   Pasture, Higher Gerwill, 9 ac.;   Meadow, Lower Gerwill, 5 ac.;   Pasture, Cross Parke, 5 ac.;   Meadow, called 'the above home', 7 ac.;   Meadow, called Little Parke, 3 ac.;   Pasture, called Lambes Parke, 4½ ac.;   'moorish ground' called the Moore, 5 ac.;   Pasture, called Little Lambes Parke, 2½ ac.;   'with the profits and herbage of three lanes called Greene Lane, Velingbridge Lane and Gerwill Lane.
Acres in toto with the scite of the house 60.'

Granted by indenture by King Charles when Prince of Wales, 12 Dec. 1621 to Christopher Trehane of St Udy alias St Tudy gent. Term: 99 years on lives of John Westlake jn. (42), Frances W. (35), and Nicholas W. (33). Heriot £2. Rent £2 17s. Impr. val. £42.
Exceptions, etc.; 'they are bound not to plow or eare up any meadow ground, auntient pasture ground, sheepe walkes or greensward . . . but the same to continue as they then were.' To plant 6 trees yearly. Lease assigned 13 Dec. 1621 to John Westlake sn., gent. J. W. left the premises by will to Francis W., his s. and one of the 'lives', who is now in possession.
Trees now growing are worth £6.

'DEMEASNES LAND HELD BY COPPIE'
Katherin Mayow (54) and Joseph Mayou (28) her s., by copy of 31 Aug. 1627: 2 closes in Overpoole Parke of 11 ac. Term: lives successively. Heriot 1s 8d. Fine at lord's will. Rent 8s. Impr. val. £10.

William Webber (35) and Nicholas W. (32), sons of Richard W. of Bodmin, by copy of 3 Oct. 1636: close called Overpoole Park of 12 ac. Term: lives successively. Heriot 1s 8d. Fine as above. Rent 8s. Impr. val. £10 10s.
Stephen Tooker (dec.), John T. (3) and Susan T. (32) his s. and d., by copy of 5 Oct. 1640: close called the Lower Poole Parke of 11 ac. Term: lives successively. Heriot 1s 8d. Fine as above. Rent 13s 4d. Impr. val. £8 14s.

Thomas May (dec.), Thomas M. (40) and James M. (37) his sons, by copy of 18 Sept. 1634, close called Poole Parke of 10 ac. Term: lives successively. Heriot and fine, as above. Rent 13s 4d. Impr. val. £8 10s.

William Rowse (dec.) and Humphrey R. (44), by copy of 29 Aug. 1612, 2 closes called Downe Parke of 23 ac. Term: lives successively. Heriot and fine, as above. Rent 8s 4d. Impr. val. £11 10s.

John Tomlyn (dec.), Thomas T; (dec.) his s. and Walter T. (71) s. of Thomas, by copy of 28 July 1580, ⅛ of 8 closes called Downe Parkes of 8 ac. Heriot and fine, as above. Rent 4s 2d. Impr. val. £5.
Reversion granted 31 July 1627 to Elizabeth Tomlyn (46) w. of Philip T. for life.

Greenevile Hawke (19), Josias H. (17) and Gartride H. (20), by copy of 5 June 1634 2 closes called Downe Parkes of 10 ac. Heriot and fine, as above. Rent 4s 2d. Impr. val. £5 5s.

John Congdon sn. (dec.), John C. jn. (60) and Jane (5) his w., by copy of 29 Aug. 1612 moiety of close called Bigger Downe Parke of 20 ac. Heriot and fine, as above. Rent 8s 4d. Impr. val. £11.

Thomas Congdon (dec.) and Humphrey C. (58), sons of John C., by copy of 29 Aug. 1634, 2 closes called Downe Parke of 20 ac. Term: lives successively. Heriot and fine, as above. Rent 8s 4d. Impr. val. £11.

Robert Horwell (dec.), Margerie (dec.) his w. and Marrian Evans (50) their d., by copy of 28 Oct. 1613, 20 rods of waste land in a common at Dunnowes Poole 'for the building of a house to inhabite in conteyninge in length 24 foote and in breadth 12 foote.' Term: lives successively. Heriot and fine, as above. Rent 1s 8d. Impr. val. 8s 4d.

Launcellott Tomlyn (32) s. of Walter T. (dec.), by copy of 17 May 1622, 2 closes called Brome Parkes of 7 ac. Heriot and fine, as above. Rent 2s 4d. Impr. val. £1.

Thomas Tomlyn (dec.) and Walter T. (72) his s., by copy of 28 July 1580, third of close called Broome Parke of 15 ac. Heriot and fine, as above. Rent 4s 8d. Impr. val. £2 5s.
Reversion granted 31 July 1627 to Elizabeth T. (46) w. of Philip.

John Tome (64) s. of Peter T., by copy of 29 Aug. 1612, third of close called Pentire Parke of 10 ac. Term, for life. Heriot and fine, as above. Rent 8s 10¾d. Impr. val. £8 10s.
Reversion granted 5 May 1634 to Peter T. (34) and John T. (27), sons of John T. for lives.

Josias Rolle gent. (dec.) and James Bligh gent. (42) and Elizabeth B. (40) s. and d. of Richard B. gent. (dec), by copy of 29 Aug. 1612, 2 parts of a close called Pentire Parke of 20 ac. Term: lives successively. Heriot and fine, as above. Rent 17s 9½d. Impr. val. £16.

John Westlake jn. (42), Francis W. (35) and Nicholas W. (33), sons of John W. sn., by copy of 17 May 1622, quarter of a close called Furse Parke of 16 ac. Term: lives successively. Heriot and fine, as above. Rent 4s. Impr. val. £2 9s.

The same, of the same date, third of 2 closes called Broome Parke of 7½ ac. Term: lives successively. Heriot and fine, as above. Rent 2s 4d. Impr. val. £1 7s.

FREEHOLDERS OF THE MANOR

Anthony Nicoll esq., ten. in Tregerricke [Tregarrick], 19s 4d; John Billinge esq., ten. in Nether Tregerricke, 1s 1d; William Hitchins, ten. in Stamquite alias Tamsquite [Tamsquite in St Tudy], 1s 5d; Heirs of Nicholas Raw gent., moiety of ten. in Stamquite, 11d; John Kestle gent., the other moiety, 11d; Heirs of Robert Scawen gent., Moiety of ten. in Stamquite, 11d; Humphrey May, the other moiety, 11d; *id.*, 4 ac. in Stamquite, 2d; William Hickes, ten. in Stamquite, 1s; Heirs of John Craddocke, ten. in Hender [or Hendra], 12s; Lady Jane Carew, 'the Bayliwicke' of the Manor of Penpoint [Penpont in St Kew], 12s; Heirs of John Grills kt. and Stephen Tooker gent., lands in Lewarne, 1s; Heirs of Thomas Robbins, ten. in Trewardale, 6d; Thomas Porter clerk, close called Longfurse Close, 1s; *id.*, 'a lane called the Watering Lane', 6d.

Total rents of assize 52 8d.

Md. 'that there is paid by the Reeve of the Mannor unto Mr Billinge yearely for a head weare the rent of twelve pence soe that the rents of assize aforesaid are de claro' p.a. 51s 8d.

'COPPIE-HOLDERS FOR LIVES WITHIN THE SAID MANNOR'

John Chapman (dec.) and Lewis C. (30) his s., by copy of 31 July 1627, ten. in Colesent [in St Tudy] of 29 ac. Term: lives successively. Heriot: a best beast. Fine, at the lord's will. Rent 16s 9½d. Impr. val. £16 10s. Farlieu 20s.

William Kempthorne (40) s. of John K., and Phillipa his w. (40), by copy of 18 Oct. 1622, 2 ten. in Loskeyle [in St Tudy] of 75 ac. Term: lives. Fine, heriot and farlieu, as above. Rent 41s 7d. Impr. val. £50.

Richard Kempthorne (dec.), Elizabeth his w. (60) now w. of Richard Tamly, and Richard K. (30) s. of John K., by copy of 22 Jan. 1619, ten. in Colesent of 37 ac. Term: lives. Fine, heriot and farlieu, as above. Rent 17s 5½d. Impr. val. £21 5s.

Thomas Hooper sn. (52) and Thomas H. jn. (31) his s., by copy of 27 Oct. 1619, ten. in Colesent of 33 ac. Term: lives. Fine, heriot and farlieu, as above. Rent 17s 5½d. Impr. val. £18 15s.

Thomason Chapple (60) wid. late w. of George C., by virtue of her widow's estate, ten. called Pendrew alias Pendreve in Blisland of 35 ac. Term: her widowhood. Fine, heriot and farlieu, as above. Rent 26s 9½d. Impr. val. £16 3s.
Reversion granted 18 Sept. 1612 to Thomas C. (48) and Henry C. (dec.), sons of George C. for their lives.

Joan Symons (80) wid., w. of Gabriel S., in virtue of her widow's estate: ten. in Penhale [*id.* in St Tudy] of 22½ ac. Term: her widowhood. Fine, heriot and farlieu, as above. Rent 16s 9½d. Impr. val. £11.
Reversion granted 10 Oct. 1617 to William Symons (44) and Joan (37) his w. Term: lives.

Walter Wills (40) and Humphrey W. (20), s. of Humphrey W., by copy of 3 Oct. 1640, ten. in Penhale of 25 ac. Term: lives. Fine, heriot and farlieu, as above. Rent 17s 3½d. Impr. val. £14 19s.

Richard Cooke (dec.), Patience (dec.) his w. and John (53) their s. by copy of 12 Oct. 1598, ten. in Penhale of 25 ac. Term: lives. Fine, heriot and farlieu, as above. Rent 16s 8½d. Impr. val. £15 4s.

William Symons (dec.) and Walter S. (40), by copy of 22 Oct. 1635, 2 ten. in Tregooden [in St Tudy] of 77 ac. Term: lives. Fine, heriot and farlieu, as above. Rent £2 11s 7½d. Impr. val. £43 14s.

Stephen Tooker (dec.) and John (30) his s., by copy of 18 July 1640, ten. called Hendra Magna [Hendra in St Tudy] and moiety of a close called Hendra Downe 'in severall closes conteyning in the whole 47 acres.' Term: lives. Fine, heriot and farlieu, as above. Rent £1 0s 9½d. Impr. val. £19 17s. Margerie T. (58) wid., late w. of Stephen T., has possession by virtue of her widowhood.

[Defaced in P.R.O. copy] The same, of the same date, ten. called Hendraparva of 24 ac. Term: lives successively. Fine, heriot and farlieu, as above. Rent 12s 4½d. Impr. val. £10 3s. Margerie, as above, has possession during her widowhood.

Johan Pawley (dec.) and John (50) his s., by copy of 18 Sept. 1622, ten. of 7 ac. with a corn mill and a course of water to it and mulcture of all the tenants of the manor, called Tynten Mill. Fine, heriot and farlieu, as above. Rent £1 6s 8d. Impr. val. £10 14s.

Francis Westlake (32) and Nicholas W. (28) sons of John W., by copy of 27 May 1633, ten. called Over Redviall [Redvale in St Tudy] of 20 ac. and ten. called Little Redviall of 2 ac. Term: lives. Fine, heriot and farlieu, as above. Rent 15s 5½d. Impr. val. £13 13s.

Thomas Lukey sn. (74), Nicholas L. (40) and Thomas L. jn. (30), by copy of 13 June 1624, ten. of Hendra of 52 ac. Term: lives. Fine, heriot and farlieu, as above. Rent 10s 3¾d. Impr. val. £9.

Chamond Greenevill (27) and Grace G. (dec.) s. and d. of Richard G. of Norcott [Northcott in Poughill], by copy of 30 April 1627, 2 ten. in Tresquare [in St Tudy] of 92 ac. Term: lives. Fine, heriot and farlieu, as above. Rent £2 8s 3½d. Impr. val. £45 16s.

Phillippa Nicholl (62) wid., in virtue of her widow's estate, ten. in Tregarricke of 33 ac. Term: her widowhood. Fine, heriot and farlieu, as above. Rent £1 0s 9½d. Impr. val. £14 4s.

Margerie Congdon (dec.) and Margarett C. (35) ds. of John C. (60) by copy of 19 April 1621, hold reversion of ten. in Bodrigan [in St Tudy] of 32 ac., lately occupied by John C. Term: lives. Fine, heriot and farlieu, as above. Rent 14s 9½d. Impr. val. £16 18s.

Thomas Tomlyn (dec.) and Walter T. (72) his s., by copy of 28 July 1580, ten. in Wringford of 42 ac. Term: lives. Fine, heriot and farlieu, as above. Rent £1 2s 9½d. Impr. val. £25.

Edward Pawley (37), by copy of 10 Oct. 1640, ten. in Bodrigan of 26½ ac. Term: life. Fine, heriot and farlieu, as above. Rent 14s 9½d. Impr. val. £16 18s.

John Gonne sn. (dec.), John G. (50) and Hercules G. (dec.), by copy of 29 Aug. 1612, ten. in Bodrigan of 39 ac. Term: lives. Fine, heriot and farlieu, as above. Rent 14s 9½d. Impr. val. £22 12s. John G. jn. is in possession.

'TENEMENTS IN HAND AND AT THE PRESENT DISPOSALL OF THE LORD'
3 ten. called Trenarlett [*id.* in St Tudy] and a cott. in Penhale, previously let by copy to John Foote gent. and Richard Foote jn. for lives, both of whom are dead, 90 ac. in all. Impr. val. £52. Md. that the above was lately in the possession of Margarett Foote (dec.), wid. of John F., and was occupied after her death by Walter Fitzwilliams who married the d. and heiress of John and Margaret F. Rent, when let by copy, had been £3 10s 4½d. Trees on the ten. are worth £4.

Trees on William Kempthorne's ten. are worth £6, and those on Tinten Mill, occupied by John Pawley, £3 10s.
There are 10½ ac. of wood of 20 years' growth on the ten. of John Congdon, John Gunn, Edward Pawley, Thomas Hooper and Richard Tomlyn, worth £63.

'THE BOUNDES OF THE SAID MANNOR
The said Mannor . . . is bounded to a bridge called Venver [Wenford] Bridge by the land of John Billing esq. and from thence by a river called the River Allen on the east side; on the south side with a mannor called Tresarrett [in St Mabyn] sometimes the land of John Trelawney barronett and now in the possession of John Rowe esq.; on the west side with the mannor of Trevisquite [in St Mabyn] being the lands of Richard Lewis esq., and the mannor of Kellegreene [Kellygreen in St Tudy], being the lands of John Wollacombe esq. and on the north side with the mannor of St Tudy, being the lands of Anthony Nicholl esq.'

OFFICERS WITHIN THE SAID MANOR
A steward, chosen by the lord, is to hold the court leet twice yearly and the court baron as often as is necessary. A reeve is chosen at Michaelmas.
A tithing man is chosen 'who is to doe suite to the Hundred Court and to pay a certeine rent out of the said mannor called smoke silver.'
Six tenants are chosen to be 'viewers of reparacions'.

THE CUSTOMS OF THE MANOR
Relief and heriot are paid.
Widows may continue to occupy their late husbands' tenement, but not the widows of tenants of Barton lands.
A tenant in occupation is 'to have the refuse of takeing a revercionall estate of any of the tenements he holds before any other shalbe admitted. And if a tenement fall in hand the next in blood to the last tenant which died in possession ought to have the refuse thereof.'
A surrender should be made in court before the Steward and some of the tenants.

Growing timber may be used on any tenement for repairs. A tenance may sublet from year to year.

'. . . if any tenement . . . fall in hand, the lord being under age and thereby not capable of settinge out the same, the partie whom the last tennant that died in possession shall nominate ought to hold the same at halfe profitts till a coppie may conveniently by graunted.'

ABSTRACT OF THE PRESENT RENTS

Rents of assize and perquisites	£5　5s
Rents of the Barton	£2　17s
Rents of copyhold land of the Barton	£5　17s　8¼d
Rents of copyhold land of the Manor	£21　13s　3¼d
Value of tenements and cottage in hand	£52
	Total £87　12s　11½d

Improved value of the Barton	£42
ditto of Barton copyhold tenements	£113　8s　8d
ditto of Manorial copyhold tenements	£412　15s
	Total £568　3s　8d

Value of timber	£19　10s
Value of woods and underwood	£63

'This is an exact survey . . .'

45　MANOR OF TREGAMERE

DCO S/4; PRO E 317 (C)/48. This small, fragmented manor lay in the parish of St Columb Major. It was acquired by the Duchy in 1540 as part of the lands of Henry Courtenay, Marquis of Exeter.

'A Survey of the Mannor of Tregamere . . . retorned [3 April 1650].

FREE-TENNANTS OF THE SAID MANNOR

John Vivian esq. holdeth freely to him and his heires for ever in soccage one tenement called Treverne and one 'Bedum' Mill [*see* p. vi] in Tregamere for which he paieth' 13s 4d.

id.: ten. in Trewan [*id.*], 1s;　John Smith of Padstowe, in right of his w., lands called Georges Close, 2s;　Sir John Arundell, ten. in Treganhatham, 10d;　John　Vivian　esq.,　ten.　called　Trewornicke　[Trevornick], 1s 8d;　[J—] Moyle, ten. called Rosavanion [Rosevanion], 1s 3d.

Total £1 0s 1d

COPYHOLDERS FOR LIVES

Rachell Arundell (dec.), William A. (50) and Thomas A. (55) her sons, by copy of 20 Oct. 1618, ten. called Trewithicke [Trevithick] of 31 ac. Term: lives successively. Fine, at the Lord's will. Rent 20s. Impr. val. £15 9s.

William Trekene (dec.) and Thomas T. (40) his s., by copy of 12 Aug. 1619, ten. in Tregameere of 20 ac. Term, as above. Fine, as above. Rent 10s 10d. Impr. val. £12.

Honor Trekene (about 60), late w. of William T., is in possession in virtue of her widow's estate.

John Vivian (33) and Thomas V. (31), sons of John V., by copy of 16 May 1634, a moiety of a corn mill called Tregameere Mill with a course of water and suit of mulcture. Term, as above. Fine, as above. Rent 3s 4d. Impr. val. £4 17s.

Francis Vivian (26) and Mathew V. (24), sons of John V. esq., by copy of 16 May 1634, moiety of a ten. in Tremaine [Tremayne] of 32 ac. Term, as above. Fine, as above. Rent 11s 8d. Impr. val. £13 1s.

Thomas Carthew (dec.), John C. (36) and Peter C. (32), by copy of 12 Aug. 1619, ten. in Tregameere of 20 ac. Term, as above. Fine, as above. Rent 10s 10d. Impr. val. £9 6s.

'The Mannor lieth in the Parish of Columbe Major but being intermixed and severed with other lands, it cannot be distinctly bounded.'

CUSTOMS

Two courts leet and two courts baron are held yearly. Customary tenants serve in turn as reeve.

Free and conventionary tenants pay respectively a relief and a heriot, and customary tenants 20s upon every surrender for a 'farlieue'.

The reeve to collect fines, amerciaments, etc., which amount on average to 6s.

A widow may continue to hold her late husband's tenement.

ABSTRACT

Rents of assize and perquisites	£1 6s 1d
Rents of copyhold tenants	£2 16s 8d
Total	£4 2s 9d
Improved value of the copyhold tenements after the lives are expired	
	£2 14s 3d

'This is an Exact Survey . . .'

46   MANOR OF TRELOWIA

DCO S/4; PRO E 317 (C)/49. The manor lay in the parishes of Morval and St Martin by Looe. It was acquired by the Duchy in 1540, and had previously been part of the lands of Henry Courtenay, Marquis of Exeter.

'A Survey of the Mannor of Trelowia . . .retorned [25 January 1649/50].

FREEHOLDERS

John Moyle gent. holdeth in free soccage to him and his heires for ever certeine lands in Trewalla by . . . two suits yearly to the Lords courtes'.

Heirs of Mr Carew, land called Treledrin by the same service; Walter Langdon, 'a certain cottage', by the same service; Stephen Medulysh clerk, ten. and 40 ac., suit to two courts and 1d.

COPYHOLDERS FOR LIVES

Thomas Hoskin (dec.), William Hill (57) and Emma Hill (dec.) his w., by copy of 19 Dec. 1617, ten. in Trelowya and 60 ac. Term: lives successively. Fine, at the lord's will. Rent 27s 8d. Impr. val. £28 8s.

There is now at the Lord's disposal 3 ac. of wood of 7 years' growth on part of this land, worth 20s per ac., 60s.

John Evans (dec.) sn., John Evans (30) his s. and Barbara (30) w. of the latter, by copy of 26 Jan. 1616, ten. in Trelowya of 30 ac. Term: lives successively. Fine, as above. Rent 13s 4d. Impr. val. £12.

There is on the tenement 1 ac. of wood of 7 years' growth, worth £8 10s.

Daniell Little (33), Margerie (33) his w. and Priscilla (60) m. of David L., by copy of 13 Oct. 1641, cottage in Hessenford [*id.*] and a close called Tookeing Mill Parke of 3 ac., and a fulling mill with a weir called Welly Weare. Term and fine, as above. Rent 5s 8d. Impr. val. £5.

There is on the tenement 2½ ac. of wood of 7 years' growth worth 20s per ac., £2 10s.

Jane Andrew (58) wid., John A. (29) and George A. (dec.), sons of George A. (dec.), by copy of 8 May 1633, a corn mill in Hessenford. Term and fine, as above. Rent 26s 8d. Impr. val. £11.

The same hold by copy of 3 Dec. 1633, ten. in Trelowya of 30 ac. Term and fine, as above. Rent 13s 4d. Impr. val. £12. There is on the ten. 4 ac. of wood at 20s per ac., £4.

LEASE-HOLDERS

Walter Evans, by L. P. of 9 May 1627, mess. or ten. in Trelowya of 60 ac. Term: 99 years on lives of Walter E. (dec.), Joan (46) and Margerie (30), children of W. E. Heriot 26s 8d. Rent 26s 8d. Impr. val. £26 6s 9d. Exceptions, etc.; to plant 6 trees yearly.

William Oliver, by L. P. of 11 March 1626, mess. or ten. in Trelowya of 60 ax., for lives of W. O. (48), Sarah (47) his w. and Edward (dec.) his bro. Heriot 26s 8d. Rent 26s 8d. Impr. val. £26 6s 9d. Exceptions etc.; to plant 4 trees yearly.

Walter Langdon gent. claims to hold 'a certeine hedge with a peece of wast ground . . . about halfe an acre by the yearely rent of 4d' for which no lease was produced. Impr. val. 5s.

[BOUNDS]

'The said Mannor is thus bounded: From a water in the highway which runneth under Treloya Church bridge on the west to Mr Modulph's land and from there by the highway which leadeth into Morvale [Morval] parish, and thence by the hedge of John Andrewes unto the land of John Hill, and from thence on the south west side by the lands of the Marquesse of Winton, and from thence by the land of Walter Langdon esq. to Seaton river, and by that river unto a hedweare belonging to the said Langdon, and thence by a leate of water unto Trewerry Wood, parte of the Mannor of Bucklawren Buck, and thence by the said leate unto the foresaid church bridge where it began'.

CUSTOMS

Two courts leet and two courts baron are held yearly. A reeve to be chosen and to collect the perquisites, which amount on average to 6s 8d.

If an estate falls in hand, the tenant 'is to hold it paying the halfe value and to take lease on halfe value for the same in case he be not able to pay the fine, and noe other is to take except the tennant doe refuse to give tenn yeares value for the renewinge the estate'. Copyholders pay a heriot on each death.

ABSTRACT

Rents of assize and perquisites	6s 9d
Rents of copyhold tenants	£4 6s 8d
Rents of leasehold tenants	£2 13s 8d
	[Total] £7 7s 1d
Improved value of copyhold tenements	£72 12s 8d
Improved value of leasehold tenements	£55 11s 10d
	[Total] £128 4s 8d[1]
Woodland on the manor is worth	£9 18s 10d

'This is an Exact Survey . . .'

47 MANOR OF TRELUGAN

DCO S/4; PRO E 317 (C)/50. The manor lay in the parish of Gerrans, but included land as far away as Constantine parish. It was acquired by the Duchy in 1540, and had previously been part of the lands of Henry Courtenay, Marquis of Exeter.

'A Survey of the Mannor of Trelugan . . . retorned [30 March 1950].

FREE-HOLDERS OF THE SAID MANNOR

John Arundell of Trerice, John Penhallow of Philie [Philleigh parish] and the heirs of John Marton hold in free soccage to them and their heirs for ever a tenement called Tregarrow for which they pay' 2s 4d.

Hugh Trevanyon gent., ten. in Trelugan, 2s 4d; George Jago, ten. called Matheras, 1s 4d; Richard Carew de Anthony esq., Edwarth Coswarth esq. and Richard Erisy esq. in knight service, ten. in the parish of Constantine called Tregontellan [Tregantallan], 1s; Samuell Pendarvas esq. in knight service, ten. in Constantine called Trevias [Trevease], 3s 4d; Richard Rutter clerk, John Trelugan and John Polkinhorne gent., in knight service, ten. in Constantine called Treculliack [Treculliacks], 2s; Robert Wenwarne esq., in knight service, ten. called Tregoffe, 1s 3d; Samuell Pendarvas esq., in knight service, ten. called Treworgan, 1s; Thomas Treuran jn., in knight service, ten. called Trewardrevah [Trewardreva in Constantine], 1s 3d.

Total rents of assize 15s 10d.

COPYHOLDERS FOR LIVES

Hanaball Randall (52), by copy of 12 Sept. 1599, mess. or ten. called Trethellans alias Trethelland of 74 ac. Term: life. Fine, at the lord's will. Rent 20s. Impr. val. £29.

---

[1] An error in arithmetic; should be £128 4s 6d.

Reversion granted to John R. (25), eldest s. of Hanaball R., 12 Nov. 1625, for life. Second reversion granted to Thomas R. (24), second s. of H. R., 2 Nov. 1627.

Gillian Nicholls wid., late w. of John N. (dec.), ten. in Trelugon of 37 ac. for her widowhood 'and noe longer'. Fine, as above. Rent 21s. Impr. val. £19 3s 6d.

Hugh Trevanion gent. claims the reversion after the death of G. N. by virtue of an order under the hands of Barkeshire, Ralphe Hopton, Edward Hide, Charles Berkeley, Robert Long and Thomas Cooke, commissioners of the late Prince for the Dukedom, whereby the Steward was ordered upon payment of £100 as a fine to grant the estate of the premises by copy to him in reversion for the term of his life and those of Hugh T. and Charles T. his sons. Half the fine was to be paid by Michaelmas 1646. This was paid to John Havers, Deputy Receiver. The second moiety was tendered by H. T. to Havers on the day appointed.

Edward Leonard (dec.), Hugh (dec.) his s. and Elizabeth (60) his d., by copy of 18 Sept. 1587, ten. in Trelugan of 36 ac., for lives. Fine, as above. Rent 16s. Impr. val. £20 17s 6d.

Katherine (60) w. of H. L. has possession during her widowhood. Reversion granted 26 Jan. 1620 to John L. (40) s. of Hugh L. for life.

John Robins (61) and George Robins (dec.), by copy of 26 Jan. 1620, ten. in Trelugan of 51 ac., for lives successively. Fine, as above. Rent 28s. Impr. val. £34 1s 6d.

John Tristeane in the parish of St Gerrance [St Gerrans], by indenture of 2 Oct. 1632, under the seal of the late King when Prince of Wales and Duke of Cornwall, ten. called Edon alias Odon in Trelugan of 48 ac. Term: 99 years on lives of Alice T. (56) his sister, William T. (dec.) s. of Adam T. of Phillie [Philleigh], Martin Rattenbury (30) of Okehampton. Heriot £4 to be paid within 28 days of the death of any 'life'. Rent 24s. Impr. val. £23 4s.

Exceptions, etc.; 'not to plough or eare up any of the meadow ground, antient pasture or greenesward . . . to plant the quantity of two acres of ground with such convenient number of oake, ash, elme or apple trees as the same will conteyne.'

Johan Kempe wid., relict and administratrix of Nicholas K. her hbd., has possession, which she claims by virtue of an assignment made by John Tristeane to her hbd. Johan K. also claims the reversion by L. P. of 19 June, 1627. Term: 99 years on the lives of Nicholas K. (dec.), John K. (28) his s. and Thomasin K. (dec.) his d.

THE BOUNDS OF THE SAID MANOR

The Manor is bounded on the east with the sea, on the south with Tregarrow [Cargurrel in St Gerrans], on the west with Metheras [Merrose in St Gerrans] and on the north with Trewothall [Treworthal].

THE CUSTOMS OF THE MANOR

Two courts leet and two courts baron are held yearly. The reeve is to be chosen at the court leet held at Michaelmas. The duties of the reeve are to collect fines, waifs, estrays, etc., worth on average [6s 8d].[1]

[1] Amount omitted in Duchy copy of the Survey.

A heriot is paid to copyholders. Widows have the right to posses their late husbands' tenements during their widowhood.

ABSTRACT

Rents of assize and perquisites of court	£1 2s 6d
Rents of copyhold tenants	£4 5s
Rents of leasehold tenants	£1 4s 10d
	Total £6 12s 4d
Improved value of copyhold lands	£103 2s 6d
Improved value of leasehold lands	£23 4s

'This is an exact survey . . .'

48   HONOUR AND MANOR OF TREMATON

DCO S/5; PRO E 317 (C)/51. The manor and honour of Trematon formed part of the ancient possessions of the Duchy. The manor occupied the western part of the parish of St Stephen by Saltash. It was bordered by the borough of Saltash (No. 36).

'A Survey of the Honor and Mannor of Trematon . . . retorned [7 October 1650]

TREMATON CASTLE

The capitall messuage or mansion house of the said Honor and Mannor is knowne and called by the name of Trematon Castle, which is scituate in the Parish of Stephens juxta Salt Ash . . . which said castle was the auntient seate of the Earles of Cornewall (those that held of the Honor of the said castle in knight service were bound to repaire every one his parte thereof according to the number of knights fees by which they held). But now the said castle is out of repaire, there being hardly any thing there left but the very walls onely at the south side there standeth one old ruined house (very much in decay) consistinge of foure roomes in which the keeper of the castle liveth; wherein alsoe he keepeth the prisoners that are arrested within the said Honor or Mannor, and in which both the courtes for that parte of the Honor and Mannor which lieth in the countie of Cornewall are usually kept. On the south east side of the said house standeth a barne of two bayes of buildinge (heretofore a chaple), neare to which at the east end is a gate for entrance into the said castle, over which there hath beene divers roomes which are now torne downe and the leade that covered them carried away, the outsides onely remayninge. At the northside of the said castle standeth on a stepe mount the outsides of an old tower, the coveringe of which is alsoe taken away, by which meanes the walls are full of many gaping chinkes which threaten the ruine thereof if not repaired.

The scite of the said castle as well within the walls as without in the ditches conteyneth about three acres land nigh unto the said castle, viz on the north and east sides there lyeth a raged peece of ground knowen by the name of the Warren, conteyninge about three acres, and on the northwest side lieth two little meadowes conteyninge about three acres, and on the west and south sides of the said meadowes and castle lyeth a certeine peece of arrable ground called the Deane Parke, conteyninge twelve acres.

The agistment of which parke, meadowes, warren, scite of the castle and office of keeper of the said castle are lett by leters pattents of the late King beareing date at Westminster [19 June 1626] . . . unto Richard Carew esq. his executors and assignes [to hold] for and dureing the terme of fouerscore and nineteene yeares [on the lives of] Grace Carew (50) wife of the said Richard Carew, Alexander Carew (dec.) and John Carew (28) his sonnes . . . [Rent 26s 8d] Heriot 26s 8d. Impr. val. £20. Exceptions, etc.; to plant one tree yearly.

Lands held of the said Honor by Knights Service as well within the County of Cornewall as Devon, with the services that the occupiers (being present tennants) ought to doe for the same, and alsoe the rents they ought to pay are as follow:[1]

All that third parte of the Honor of the said Castle, viz. one and twentie knights fees in Beareferris [Bere Ferrers], Badisson, Salcombe alias Saw-combe, Bymondham, Longstone, Bediford, Newton [Newton Ferrers], and Trehenna, held heretofore by Robert Willoughby Lord Brooke by knights service (that is to say by hommage and fealtie) payinge therefore yearely at the feast of Michaell the Arch Angel two and twentie pence; and alsoe to doe suite to the Lord courtes held for the said Honor from three weekes to three weekes; likewise to keepe in good repaire one and twenty garretts of the said castle at theire owne chardges, and in time of warr to finde one and twentie men compleately armed for the keepeing of the said castle fortie daies. But if it be necessary for the said men to stay there longer that then they should be kept at the Lords chardges. Alsoe when any tennants thereof die theire heires within age shalbe in warde to the Lord. But if the said heires shalbe at full age that then the Lord shall take into his owne hand all the lands and tenements of the said heires, and shall receave all the incomes and profitts thereof until the said heire shall doe homage. And lastly the said heires are to give for every knights fee held in mortmaine five markes, and for every knights fee held in escuage twentie five shillings: 22d.

4 knights fees in Apple Downeford, Rathevile, Tregantell [Tregantle in Antony] and Brothicke, 8d; 1 fee in Trevigan, 2d; 2 fees in Lanladron alias Nansladron and St Goran, 4d; 1 fee in Killigrew [in St Erme], 2d; ½ fee in East Desard, 1d; ½ fee in Trewin, 1d; ½ fee in Callilonde, 1d; 4 fees in Halton [in St Dominick], Pilaton [Pillaton], Hardenfast, and Nod-deterre [Notter], 8d; 6 fees in Karkeele, Tregatha, Harstone, Haneknowle [Honicknowle in Plymouth] and Penhangell, 12d; 1 fee in Kings Stanton and Sutton Vateor Marie [Sutton Valletorte in Plymouth], 2d; 4 fees in Bickberrie, Lifton, Earth Grove, Notte Downe, Hughampton, and Holewell, 8d; 1 fee in Orchadon, 2d; 2 fees in Wineston, Badiston and Saltcombe [Salcombe?], 4d; ½ fee in Tregantle and Combe, 1d; ½ fee in Tregantle and Combe, 1d; 3 fees in North Ludbrooke, Yedmeston, Dun-combe alias Dawcombe, South Ludbrooke, Langham, and Trethinnett alias Trethinnicke, 6d; 2 fees in Leypunston, Lopperige [margl. Loprigr.] and Torrige, 4d; 2½ fees in Torrepicke als Prycke, Spidlescombe [Sprid-dlecombe] and Trenalward, 5d; 2 fees in Herford and Trenalowen, 4d.

---

[1] The identification of the knights' fees of the Honour of Trematon presents considerable difficulties, as they were widely scattered over eastern Cornwall and western Devon. Lists of Knights' fees between 1303 and 1428 are given in *Inquisitions and Assessments relating to Feudal Aids*, Vol. 1, Record Commission, 1899.

The water and river of Tamar, viz. from Morwilham [Morwellham] to Penley Will, Shitliston and Worston in Plym is held by 1½ fees, but is sold to the town of Saltash, 'the same being in the Lords hands' Also the Manor of Calistocke (Calstock) is held by 1 fee, but is in the Lord's hand, and is 'sould to divers persons'.

Total rents of tenants by knight service   8s 2d.

Md. 'that we cannott finde whoe are the present tennants in fee of the foresaid lands . . . nor what alienacions have happened within the saime Honor for that wee had not nor could obteyne any law records to direct us.

The farme of the relieffes of this Honor of the Castle of Launceston and the Honor of Bradninch in Comitate Devon are lett by letters pattents from the late King to one Bird under the yearely rent of [£7] but the said lease was not produced to us, neither hath the rent aforesaid beene paide since the putting downe of the Courte of Wardes because the tennants thereof have refused to pay theire relieffes. But if the said relieffes be paid within this Honor of Trematon they will amount unto [on average] £8.

This Honor of Trematon lieth dispersed into divers partes within the Counties of Cornewall and Devon, wherein the Bayliffe of the said Honor whoe holds his place in fee hath power by himselfe or his deputies to arrest any one for any some of money whatsoever which is determinable within the courte of the said Honor, which said Courte is kept every three weekes and unto which the said tennants in fee are bound to doe theire suite. The perquisites of which courte will amount unto [on average]' £3 6s 8d.

FREEHOLDERS OF THE MANOR

Roger Porter gent., ten. called Dawleys Ten., 2d; Francis Wills, lands in Holle [Hole Farm], 2s 8d; Arthur Burrell esq., lands in Trematon, 6s 8d; Heirs of Paschoe, ⅓ of certain lands in Trematon, Francis Buller the other ⅔, 2s 8d; Heirs of Paschoe, land in Pesiswalles, 1s; *id.*, ⅓ of lands in Torr, Francis Buller, other⅔, 2½d; *id.*, ⅓ of lands in 'the burroughe of the Castle of Trematon,[2] Francis Buller, the residue, 2s 6d; *id.*, lands in Combe, 2s; *id.*, lands in Broade Trematon, 2s 8d; *id.*, lands in Trehane [Trehan], 2½d; *id.*, lands in 'the burrough of the Castle . . . and all that land called Courtneye land', 2s 2d; William Bond, certain land in Tredowne, 2s; *id.*, a ten. called Daudie Poole, 6d; Reeve of the Manor of Blofleminge [Botus Fleming], lands there 2s; Joan Bond wid., land in Borraton [Burraton], 1s; Nicholas Brookenige and Richard Wills, land previously Bickton's 8d; Richard Wills, land in Trehane, 6d; Richard Ketchwich esq., land in Trematon, 2s 8d; Pearce Edgecombe esq., of Mount Edgecombe, 'for certeine lands unknowen', 2s 9d; Richard Carew, land in Tregantle [*id.* in Antony], 1s; *id.*, mills called St Johns Mills, 6d; John Wadham gent., lands in Muttenham [Moditonham in Botusfleming], 2s; Thomas Foynes esq., lands in Hunneknowle [Honicknowle, Devon], 3d; Peter Clare, lands in Blofleminge [Botusfleming], 6d; William Crabb, lands in Salt Ash, 3d; Nicholas Batten, lands in

---

[2] Trematon was technically an incorporated borough, even though it never had more than a handful of burgesses. It is possible that the borough occupied the bailey of the castle, just as at Caws Castle, Shropshire, another example of a 'lost' castle-borough. See Maurice Beresford, *New Towns of the Middle Ages*, London, 1967, pp. 411–13.

Inse [Ince], 8d;   Roger Porter, lands in the Burrough of the Castle,
2s;   *id.*, lands in White Crosse [Whity Cross], 1s 4d;   Henry Wills, lands
in the Burrough of the Castle, 1s 2d;   Francis Buller esq., lands in Foord
[Forder], 1½d;   Heirs of Champernon, lands in Modbury [Devon],
6d;   Samuel Roles kt., Manor of Inseworke [Insworke], 6d;   Francis
Wills, lands in Burdens, Wagworthy [Wadgeworthy] and Blowesparke,
2s 3d;   Roger Hunkinge, certain lands in [blank], 2s 8d;   Heirs of John
Crocker esq., lands in Torrpeeke [Torpoint] and Springle Combe,
2s 8d;   [—] Rouse esq., lands in Halton [*id.* in St Dominick],
6d;   Nicholas Stacey, lands in the borough of the Castle, 1s;   Heirs of
John Connocke, 'all that land called Trewarde', 40s.
Total [in a different hand]   £4 14s 10½d.

CONVENTIONARY TENANTS OF INHERITANCE

Galfrey Bulley, 35 ac., part of two tenements in Little Ash, made up of a
   mess. and 86 ac. in 2 ac. C.; John Tapson, [—] Rowe wid. and Anthony
   Geepe, 30 ac.; William Hunkin, the residue. Fine £4 13s 4d. Rent 26s 8d.
Thomas Tapson, a quarry of slate in Little Ash. Fine Nil. Rent 1s.
Abraham Jennings, merchant, 2 ac. in Rockborroughe [?Borough in
   Antony], part of a mess. and 18 ac. there; Richard Peterfield, 6 ac.;
   Nicholas Wadham gent., 6 ac.; [—] Michael wid., the residue, Fine 36s.
   Rent 4s.
William Michell gent., ten. in Wharfelton. Fine 6s 7½d. Rent 2s.
William Skory, mess. and 14½ ac.; Noell Some: moiety of mess. and close
   called Elming Yate; Agnes Some, the other moiety; Alice Hunkin,
   meadow called Gripes in Attdowne alias Tredowne [Tredown]. Fine 30s.
   Rent 6s.
Edmond Herringe, close called Borrough Downe, part of a ten. in Borraton
   [Burraton]; Paule Jackeman, barn, bakehouse, garden and close called
   Backhouse Close of 1½ ac.; John Hele, house, garden and orchard;
   William Evans, house, garden and orchard; John Gatwell, house and
   garden; Thomas Bowhaie, 4 ac. in Borrough Downe; Agnes Riche, house
   and part of a garden; Johan Walter, close called Warre Parke. Fine 20s.
   Rent 6s.
Johan Wills, mess. in Borratton. Fine 20s. Rent 6s.
id., mess in Borraton. Fine 30s. Rent 6s.
id., moiety of ten. in Borraton, except a house, garden and orchard; Walter
   Pethin, the said house, garden and orchard; Ralphe Colwell, house,
   garden and moiety, part of the other moiety; Francis Crocker, third of the
   said moiety; Joan Wills wid., eighth of the moiety; Emma Barges wid.,
   house called the Backhouse; Thomas Bowhaie, a fourth part. Fine
   60s 8d. Rent 11s.
Walter Pethin, mess. in Burraton. Fine 66s 8d. Rent 11s 4d.
Joan Wills wid., ten. in Burraton. Fine 30s. Rent 5s.
William Hobbe, 6 closes in Old Tamerton of 18 ac.; Robert Hunkin, house,
   orchard and 4 ac.; Elizabeth Geddy wid., 2 closes of 4 ac.; Joan Bickton,
   house, garden, orchard and close, being the residue of the ten. Fine
   26s 9d. Rent 6s 9d.
Roger Porter, 3 closes in Old Tematon, part of a ten. of 6 ac.; Richard
   Bickton, 6 ac.; John Walter, residue. Fine 20s. Rent 6s.

William Garthe, house, garden and 2 closes and a meadow, part of ten. in Old Trematon; John Axford, a close; John Crabb, mess. and garden; Roger Bickton, a house; John Walter, the residue. Fine 20s. Rent 6s.

	Fine	Rent
John Walter, $\frac{2}{3}$ of ten. in Old Trematon; Richard Porter, the residue	1s	1s
Richard Bone, mess. in Old Trematon	30s 4½d	10s
William Hobb, mess. in Old Trematon	15s 6d	6s
William Webb, ¼ mess. in Old Trematon; Richard Seldon, a moiety; Richard Porter gent., ⅛; John Dill, the residue	16s 8d	5s 10d
Thomas Burrell esq., mess. and 25 ac. in Old Trematon	50s	16s 5d
Agnes Luce, moiety of mess. and 25 ac. in Trematon Webland; John Luce, the residue	42s 1¾d	9s 10d
John Bickton, mess. in Trematon Webland [Weblands]	11s 2½d	3s
John Roberts, mess. in Trematon Webland of 30 ac.	46s	15s 6d
William Webb, house, garden and orchard, being part of ten. in Trematon Webland; Richard Porter, the residue	24s 8d	7s 6d
John Walter jn., mess. in Trematon Webland	56s 8d	13s
Walter Pethin sn., 2 mess. in Pill [*id.*] of 40 ac.	34s	21s
Walter Pethin jn., mess. and 3 ac. in Pill	5s	2s
John Pethin, mess. and 26 ac. in Pill	40s	12s 2d
Sampson Earle, mess. in Pill	29s	7s 4d
William Hunkin and heirs and relict of John Skynn, mess. in Pill	27s	6s 6d
Joan Stephens wid., mess. and 3 ac. in Pill	6s	2s
Edmond Herring, merchant, mess. and 10 ac. in Pill	23s 6d	5s 1d
Robert Piper, mess. and 20 ac. in Pill	48s	9s 6d
Heirs of Samuell Rolles kt, mess. and 3 ac. in Pill	2s 6d	1s 2d
Marke Penny, mess. and garden in Pill	1s 6d	4d
Thomason Skin wid., cott. and garden in Pill	1s	2d
John Lang, cott. and garden in Pill	6d	2d
William Piper, cott. and 2 gardens in Pill	1s	2d
Thomas Michell, cott. and orchard in Pill	2s 6d	4d
John Bray and Tristram May, mess., garden and ½ ac. in Pill	3s	6d
Heirs of William Hawkyn and Thomas Williams, cott., garden and ½ ac. in Pill	2s	4d
Katherin Hawkin, cott. and garden in Pill	2s	4d
Thomas Raw, cott. and garden in Pill	nil	3d
Marke Hornabrooke, cott. and orchard in Pill	1s	2d
George Raw and John Cockle, 2 cott., orchard and garden in Pill	nil	3d
Nicholas Orchard, cott. and orchard in Pill	3s	8d
Christopher Reede, merchant, mess. and 5 ac. in Pill	10s	2s

	Rent		Fine	
William Crocker jn., 3 ac. in Pill	6s		1s	
Tristram Hay, 5 ac. in Pill	13s		2s	
Nicholas Wadham, mess. and 8 ac. in Pill	38s		11s	8d
Edmond Cowline, third of a moiety of mess. in Wharfelton [Warfelton]; William Stacy gent., ⅓; William Michell gent., house and close of 3 ac.; Robert Stephens, house, orchard and garden; John Glidon,⅓ of a moiety; Peter Ley, Henry Marten and John Calmady, the residue	66s	8d	13s	4d
Thomas Rowter, moiety of mess. in Wharfelton; Thomas Die, ¼; Peter Ley, Henry Marten and John Calmady, the other quarter, except a house and orchard which Richard Carter holds	66s	8d	8s	
Thomas Rowter, moiety of mess. in Wharfelton; Thomas Dier, the residue	nil		1s	
Jone Wills wid., moiety of mess. in Wharfelton; Sampson Bond, the other moiety	33s	4d	9s	
Richard Skelton, moiety of a mess. in Broadmoore [Broadmoor]; John Gliddon, the other moiety except 1 ac. which John Axford holds	30s		8s	
John Axford, moiety of mess. and 20 ac. in Broadmoore; Richard Skelton, the other moiety	30s		8s	
Nicholas Symons gent., mess. and 45 ac. in Broadmoore	60s		16s	
Alice Hunkin wid., mess. in Innes [Ince] Downe	40s		12s	
Thomas Skelton, mess. and 23 ac. in Stoken [Stoketon]	36s	10d	10s	
[—] Hickins wid., mess. and 24 ac. in Stoken	36s		10s	
Alice Hoskin and Josias Hobbe, mess. called Elming Yate in Attdowne	14s		2s	8d
Josias Hobbe, mess. in Attdowne	16s	4d	5s	4d
Thomas Bushell, garden and part of a ten. in Borraton; William Randall, a close of 1 ac.; Katherin Lavers, 1¼ ac.; John Hoskin, 4 ac.; Richard Golston, ¾ ac.; Henry Herring, 3½ ac.; William Hendy, house and close; Robert Will, residue of ten. except 35 perches which John Isaacke holds	26s	4d	5s	4d
Joan Foster wid., mess. in Greepes [Greeps]	22s		7s	2d
Thomas Bushell, garden, part of ten. in Borraton; William Randall, close of 1 ac.; Katherin Lavers, 1¼ ac.; John Hoskin, 4 ac.; Richard Golston, ¾ ac. Henry Herringe, 3½ ac.; William Hendie, house with adjoining close; Robert Will, residue except 25 perches which John Isaack holds	26s	8d	5s	4d
John Isaacke, land in Borraton	nil			4d
Edward Herringe, 11 ac. part of ten. in Borraton; Saphirus Paine, 4 ac.; Francis Crocker, residue	12s		5s	4d
John Wills wid. [sic], piece of land called Rock-borroughe Parke and another close 'by the Way side' of 10 ac., part of ten. called Cowdray and				

	Rent	Fine
Huntland; John Calmadie, residue, except ½ ac. which Nicholas Axford holds	60s	15s
Richard Carew esq., a corn mill with a fulling mill near Trematon Castle [margl. note: 'Forde Mills']	nil	53s 4d
Hitchins Wadham kt., 'certeine mills called Salt Mills'	nil	80s
id., piece of land called Normans Parke	nil	8d
William Corriton kt, 'the fishing of the Water of Linner'	nil	13s 4d
Thomas Wivell esq., mess. and ten. called Penfentell	£6	8s

The tenants give £14 8s 4d as Old Recognition money, which is paid in the first three years following every Assession, amounting on average to 41s 2¼d and a seventh of ½d

Fines paid within 6 years after every Assession are £77 6s 0½d, 'which being devided into seven partes amounts unto' on average £11 0s 11d and a seventh of ½d.

TENANTS AT WILL

John Walter, meadown called Lords Meade, for the use of the tenants of Broad Trematon, of 4 ac. Rent 4s. Impr. val. £4.

Francis Buller esq., royalties of hunting, hawking, etc. Fine 1s every 7 years. Rent 2s. Worth yearly 2s 6d.

LEASEHOLDERS

James Finch gent., by L. P. of 30 May 1625, piece of land called Justing peece alias Justing Place, and also a piece of 'void ground in Aish [Saltash] lying between the burgage late belonging to the Priory of Plimpton [Plympton, Devon] on the south and west parte and the burgage of Thomas Bickton on the north and east side'. Term: 99 years on the lives of Thomas Finch (61) of Plymouth, merchant, Elizabeth (dec.) his wife, and Elizabeth (26) their daughter. Rent of the Justing Place 2s, of the void land 1d. Impr. val. £3 18s. Exceptions, etc.

Sir John Walter, Sir James Fullerton and Sir Thomas Trevor, by L. P. of 14 June 1628, small pieces of land in Saltash, viz. (1) garden lately held by William Anthony; (2) garden in Midle Streete, lately held by Robert Barrett; (3) garden in Highstreete, lately held by Leonard Carpenter; (4) piece of land called Oble, lately held by [—] Wadham gent.; (5) garden in Trematon Borough; (6) piece of land called Pekeswall. Term: 31 years. Rent 2s 2d. Impr. val. £5 10s.

Assigned to Thomas Caldwell esq. by deed of 17 March 1629, who assigned it 31 Oct. 1630 to Richard Langford, who in turn assigned it 1 May 1633 to Sir Richard Buller. Buller assigned his right in the part called Obble to Nicholas Wadham gent. 2 May 1633. Wadham assigned it 6 April 1648 to Edmond Herringe, the present tenant. Rent 8d. Worth yearly 20s.

Sir Richard Buller, by deed of 17 Jan. 1634 assigned the garden in High Street to [—] Michell, the present tenant. Rent 2d. Worth yearly £3.

The residue is in the possession of Francis Buller esq., executor of Sir Richard Buller. Rent 1s 4d. Worth yearly 30s.

'soe that the whole improvement being thus devided amountes to the forementioned some of £5 10s beside the rent aforesaid.

'THE BOUNDES OF THE SAID MANNOR

The said Mannor cannot be precisely bounded in regard it lieth dispersed into divers quarters and partes and separate each from other, severall free lands aswell mannors as independent tenements interveninge. But the whole Mannor is confined within the parish of St Stephen juxta Salt Ash and is all inclosed in severall known all in its distinct partes by the respective tennants (in case any intrusion be offered) doe use to present it at the Law Courtes whereby all such passages are certified and soe the boundaries are kept intire and free from all incroachments'.

CUSTOMS

An Assession Court is held every seven years, a Court Baron every three weeks, and a Court Leet twice yearly. New Knowledge money, payable after the surrender of a holding, amounts on average to 46s 8d. Perquisites amount on average to £6 13s 4d. Reeve, beadle and tithingman are chosen. Widows continue to occupy their late husbands' tenements. Relief and heriot are payable.

A customary tenant 'cannot forfeite his estate by any act whatsoever and in case his rent or other duties be in arreare the Reeve for non payment is to make distresse.'

ABSTRACT

Rents of assize and perquisites	£15
Rents of leasehold tenants and tenants at will	£1 16s 9d
Rents of customary tenants	£27 13s 5d
Fines paid by customary tenants, on average	£11 0s 11d and a seventh of ½d.
Old Knowledge money, on average	£2 1s 2¼d and a seventh of ½d.
New Knowledge money	£2 6s 8d
	Total £59 18s 11¼d and a seventh of 1d.
Improved value of Honour and Manor	£41 10s 6d

'This is an exact survey . . .[sd]'

49 MANOR OF TREVENNEN

DCO S/4; PRO E 317 (C)/52. This manor lay in two widely separated parcels in the parishes of Gorran and St Erme. It came to the Dµchy in 1540 as part of the lands of the dissolved priory of St Andrew, Tywardreath.

'A Survey of the Mannor of Trevennen alias Tremaynon . . . retorned [3 April 1650]

Free tennants of the said Mannor

John Trefrie holdeth freely to him and his heires for ever in soccage one farlingate of land Cornish in Trevarrecke alias Tremvecke for which he paieth' 6d.

John Broade, William Middlecoate and Thomas Kerkine, $\frac{1}{2}$ ac. C. in Trewarrecke [Trevarrick in St Gorran], 2s; John Gregor, $\frac{1}{2}$ ac. C. in Trewarrecke, 3s; Edward Hoblin esq., William Slade and Andrew [—], $\frac{1}{2}$ ac. C. in Trevallisvegham and Trevallisvehore [Trewalla or Trewolla in St Goran], 5s 11d; Sir Charles Trevanion, $\frac{1}{2}$ ac. in Tolcarne, 5s; [—] Alworth gent, 1 farl. in Benathlacke [Benallack] in Probus parish, previously Tregian's, 2s; Sir Charles Trevanion, 1 farl. in Trevennen als Tremaynon, 3s 4d; Edward Hoblin esq., $\frac{1}{2}$ ac. C. in Trevascoyes [Trevascus in St Goran], 4s; *id.*, $\frac{1}{2}$ ac. C. in Trevallameere [Trewalla in St Goran], 18s; Nathaniel Trevanion esq., 2 closes in Travascoyes of 50 ac., 26s 8d.

William Slade and Christian Hoyle wid., mess. and lands in Tremaynon and Goodarrecke assigned by Edward Slade his f., who held by assignment from William Slade, who had it from John Slade, who married Christian Vivian, coheir of Thomas Vivian, who held it by grant from Thomas Colyn, Prior of the house and Church of St Andrew, Tywardreath, by deed of 10 July 1536, 66s 4d.

Leaseholders

Richard Hoyle of Gorran (dec.), John H. (40) and Arthur H. (dec.), by deed of King Charles when Prince of Wales, 20 Nov. 1622, messuages, land and tenements on Trewarrecke, totalling 52 ac., on their lives. Fine £109. Rent 22s. Impr. val. £26 18s. Woodland is worth £4. Exceptions, etc.; to plant 2 trees yearly.

Thomas Polwheele of Treworgan, by L. P. of 21 July 1626, mess and lands in Pengelly Prior [Pengelly in St Erme], totalling $163\frac{1}{2}$ ac. Term: 99 years on the lives of John Polwheele (43), Robert P. (dec.) and Stephen P. (28). Fine £255. Rent 40s. Heriot £4. Impr. val. £81. Exceptions, etc.; to plant 6 trees yearly.

Bounds 'This Mannor cannot be bounded in regard that it lieth soe farr distant one parte from other, Trevennen lying in the parish of Gorran and Pengelly Prior in the parish of St Erne [St Erme] tenn miles thence'.

Customs

Two courts baron and two courts leet are held yearly; at one of them the reeve is chosen.

Freeholders pay a relief, except those obligated to pay a heriot. Heriots, waifs, etc. are worth on average 6s yearly.

ABSTRACT

Rents of assize and perquisites of court	£6 12s 9d
Rents of leaseholders	£3 2s
	Total £9 14s 9d

Improved value of leasehold lands after the lives are deceased £107 18s
Woodland worth £4

'This is an Exact Survey . . .'

50   MANOR OF TREVERBYN COURTNEY

DCO S/4. There is no copy of this Survey in the Public Record Office. The manor occupied the northern part of the parish of St Austell. It came to the Duchy in 1540 as part of the lands of Henry Courtenay, Marquis of Exeter.

'A Survey of the Mannor of Treverbin Courtney . . . retorned [23 Aug. 1650].

FREEHOLDERS OF THE SAID MANNOR

The heires of William Lower holds [sic] freely to him and his heires for ever in free soccage one tenement . . . in St Austle for which he pays' 1s 1½d. Heirs of William Webb, mannor of Tregenber, 1s 1d;   Olliver Saule esq., ten. called Coynhith, 2s 2d;   Mathew Kerne, 2 parts of a ten. in St Austle Knightor [Knightor], 2s;   Heirs of Thomas Davye, ⅓ of same, 1s;   Mathew Kerne and Nicholas Gilbert, ten. in Knightor, 2s 2d;   Peter Laa, ten. called Ossover, 5s 2d;   [—] Colles, ten. called Carver [Carvear], 2s;   Sir Charles Trevanion, moiety of ten. called Carnamaninge, 1s;   Mathew Kerne, the other moiety, 1s;   Hugh Boscowen esq., ten. in St Austle called Penhendera, 3s 8d;   George Harte and Robert Harte, ten. in Hallace, 4s;   Mathew Kerne and Tho [sic] Tinner, ten. called Trethergie [Trethurgy], 1s 7½d;   William Bonde, ten. in Trethergie, 1s 7½d.
Total £1 9s 7½d.

COPYHOLDERS FOR LIVES

Oliver Saule de Penris [Penrice], by copy of 20 March 1639, ten. and 43 ac. in Carwallen in St Austell parish, for lives of Oliver (49) and Nicholas (47) his br. Rent 6s 4d. Worth £6. Reversion granted by the same copy to Robert Saule (34) of Penrice gent. for life.

Peter Boddy (70) and Ipsa Boddy (dec.) his d., by surr. of William Rowse and Richard Rowse, by copy of 7 Jan. 1623, 1 ac. C. in 42 ac. English called Treganhissey [Tregonissy], for lives. Rent 15s 3d. Worth £19 11s 9d. Reversion granted by copy of 5 May 1640 to William Slade (15), s. of Digory S. of Austle, for life.

Henry Roberts (dec.) of Tregonhissy and Peter (34) his s., by copy of 17 Oct. 1641, ten. of 45 ac. in Tregonhissy for lives. Rent 10s 3d. Worth £19 13s 3d. Christian, w. of Henry R., holds by virtue of her widow's estate.

Anne Joseph (80) wid., of John J., by reason of her widow's estate, ten of 44 ac. called Grey. Rent 15s 4d. Worth £14 8s 3d. Reversion granted by copy of 9 Oct. 1641 to Samuell Hix (40) and Samuell (10) his s. for lives.

John Hodge (35) of Carveth and Elizabeth (12) his d. by copy of 20 March 1638, ten. of 19½ ac. in Carvath for lives. Rent 15s 3d. Worth £15 12s. Reversion granted by copy of the same date to William Slade (28) of Curran.

George Roscorly (30) and John Rosecorley (26), sons of George Rosecorley, by copy of 20 Oct. 1635, ten. of 12½ ac. in Rescorley [Rescorla]. Rent 3s 4d. Worth £5 18s.
Sampson Rescorley, another s. of George R., has the reversion by copy of 23 Dec. 1635; he is 'supposed to be alive'.

William Carlyan (dec.) and Johan (50) his d., by copy of 1 June 1608, ten. of 22 ac. in Rosogon [Resugga] the Lower for lives. Rent 6s 3d. Worth £10 6s 6d. Johan is now w. of John Iland.

William Carlian (dec.) and Tristriam C. (58), sons of John Carlion of St Austell, weaver, by copy of 1 June 1608, ten. or cott. of 2 ac. in St Austell for lives. Rent 6s 8d. Worth £2 4s 4d.

John Carliam (dec.) and Tristriam aforesaid (58), by copy of the same date, 2 ten. or cotts. and 3¼ ac. in St Austell for lives. Rent 8s 5d. Worth £3.

Rose Leight (60), by widow's estate, ten. or cott. in St Austell of 1½ ac. Rent 7s 2d. Worth £1 3s 10d.

William Penhalle (60) and John P. (28), by copy of 23 Dec. 1630, ten. in Restorleigh of ½ ac. C. with 4 closes with 16 ac. English [In margin, 46 ac.], for lives. Rent 12s 7d. Worth £13.

[—] Mineheir claims an estate by copy in ten. of Benallate of 12 ac., but produced no copy. Rent 5s 2d. Worth £3 4s 4d. [Mgl. note: 'This estate to be produced'].

John Phillips make a similar claim to ten. in Penwitheck of 20 ac. Rent 6s. Worth £8 10s.

LEASEHOLDERS OF THE MANOR
Sir John Walter, Sir James Fullerton and Sir Thomas Trevor, by L. P. of 14 June 1628, ten. of 60 ac. in Rescorleigh, for 31 years. Rent 9s 9d. Worth £19. Lease assigned to Thomas Caldwell 16 March 1628. Caldwell assigned it to William Rosevear of Austle husbandman 10 May 1630.

The same, by L. P. of the same date, moiety of Treverbin Mills with 1 ac. for 31 years. Rent 7s. Worth £2 13s. The other moiety 'belongeth to an other lord'.
Lease assigned to Thomas Caldwell 27 March 1628, who assigned it to Nicholas Kendall of Luxulion gent. 14 Nov. 1629.

The same, by L. P. of the same date, ten. of 9 ac. in Menogwinner for 31 years. Rent 4s 3d. Worth £2 16s.
Lease assigned 17 [—] 1628 to Thomas Caldwell, who assigned it 20 Feb. 1631 to Richard Langford of Whitstone, who assigned it 4 May 1632 to Thomas Carne of Austle, who is now in possession.

John Boxe by indent. of 30 April 1641 has assigned to him by William Hombley gent. and Richard Bowett, fuller, ten. of 2½ ac. and a fulling mill in St Austell for residue of term of 31 years from 25 March 1628. Bowett had held by indent. of 20 July 1636 from George Cooke of Westminster, 'cord-weyner', administrator of the goods of Thomas Caldwell, which the latter had held by indent. of 17 March 1628 from Sir John Walter, etc., who had received it by L. P. of 14 June 162[—]. Rent 3s 10d. Worth £4.

John Killiow (dec.) sn., John K. jn. (70) and Ann (dec.) his w., by L. P. of 13 Feb. 159., ten. and 20 ac. in Rosogo [Resugga] for lives successively. Rent 5s 3d. Worth £4. Exceptions and allowances.

Jane Killiow wid. has the premises by assignment of 10 April 1644 from John K. jn. for 40 years if she should so long live.

Md. The ten. now in the possession of Johnson Parschoe, who claims an assignment of 17 Dec. 1640 from Richard Langford of Whitstone, to whom it was assigned by Thomas Caldwell 20 Feb. 1631, to whom it was assigned by Sir John Walter, who held it by L. P. of 14 June 1628, 'notwithstandinge the estate which Kelliow afforesaid then had and now hath therein'.

'The Boundes of the said Mannor

The said mannor is bounded on the south with the mannor of Tewington, on the west with the mannor of Trenance Austle [Trenance in St Austell] and the parish of St Stephens in Brannell, on the north with the parish of Roch [Roche], and on the east with the parish of Luxillian and the parish of St Blaysey [St Blazey].

There are divers large commons and wast grounds within the said mannor in which tennents claime right of common for there cattle unstinted, in which commons there are divers tinne mines out of which the lord hath the thirtiethe parte of a moiety for toll, except of one tinne mine knowne by the name of Greate Beame, out of which the lord hath the fifteenthe parte of the moiety for toll, and one other worke knowne by the name of Cruckeglasse, out of which the lord hath bin paide tenn shillings yearely soe that al the profitts that now acrueth to the lord (little tinne beinge wroughte in respecte the minnes doe faile) doth amount to, com. annis, £4.

Md. that wee are informed on Mr Beiley (liveing in Fleet Street London) hath L. P. for the foresaid toll tinne by which he is to paye the yearely rent of seaven pounds, but by all the information we received while we resided there, wee could hardly raise the vallue of the said toll tinne to be worth [£4 p.a.].'

Customs of the said Manor

Two courts baron and two courts leet are held yearly. Free tenants pay a relief at the rate of 12s 6d per Cornish acre. Copyholders pay a best beast as a heriot, one for each tenement. Widows of copyhold tenants may hold their late husbands' tenements for their lives. Any copyholder may 'sell or devise his coppieholde estate to home he pleaseth and into as many parts as he pleaseth'.

The Offices belonging to the Manor

A steward 'who is at the lord's disposinge and is to keepe the courts of the said mannor'.

A reeve is chosen yearly and is to collect rents, etc. and also 'as an assistant to the reeve, a tythingman who is also to doe suite to the said court'.

ABSTRACT OF THE PRESENT RENTS AND FUTURE
IMPROVEMENTS OF THE SAID MANOR

Rents of assize and perquisites	£2 16s 2½d
Toll tin	£4
Rents of copyhold tenants	£5 16s 11d
Rents of leasehold tenants	£1 10s 1d
	Total £14 3s 2½d
Improved rents of copyhold tenants	£122 12s 3d
Improved rents of leasehold tenants	£32 9s
	Total £155 1s 3d

'This is an exact survey . . . [Sd].'

51 MANOR OF TREWORGIE

DCO S/4; PRO E 317 (C)/53. The manor consisted of scattered parcels of land in St Gennys parish in North Cornwall. It had been part of the lands of the dissolved priory of St Stephen, Launceston, and was attached in 1540.

'A Survey of the Mannor of Treworgie . . . retorned [12 July 1650].

THE MANNOR MANSION OR BARTON HOUSE

The said house consisteth of one faire hall open to the roofe and wainscotted halfe way, one parlor and one kitchen below staires, and of divers Lodgeing chambers above staires. Without doores there were divers out houses for the houseing of cattle and other necessary uses which are altogether out of repaire and many of them fallen to the ground. The scite of the said house consisteth of one corte, one yard one garden and one orchard conteyninge foure acres and a halfe.

DEMEASNES LAND BELONGING TO THE SAID BARTON

All that parcell of meadow ground knowen by the name of the Way Meadow, conteyninge six acres and a halfe'; pasture called Chappell Close, 16¾ ac.; pasture called Westslade, 11 ac.; meadow called the Broade Meadow, 4 ac.; meadow known as the Little Meadow, 2¾ ac.; pasture called Horse Parke, 2¾ ac.; meadow called the Long Meadow, 6½ ac.; arable called the Windmill Hill, 5½ ac.; arable called the East Downe, 24½ ac.; arable called Middle Downe, 8½ ac.; land called Westdowne, 13½ ac.; parcel called the Downe by the Way, 10½ ac.; pasture called Longslade, 12¾ ac.; meadow called the Bottome Slade, 9 ac.; pasture called the Slade next the Comon, 3 ac.; arable called East Windmill Parke, 5½ ac.; parcel called South Parke, 5¼ ac.; arable called West Parke, 7¼ ac.; arable called North Parke, 6 ac.; meadow called Home Meadow, 2½ ac.; 'Woodground soe called', 8 ac. All with the scite of the house contain 176½ ac. Fine, at the Lord's will. Rent 52s. Impr. val. £98 14s 6d.

These premises are now occupied by Elizabeth Bligh wid. who claims to hold by L. P. of Charles I for 99 years on three lives, 'but produced not unto us the said Letters Pattents, the same being (as she saith) out of her hands for which cause we cannot certifie what condicions the lease is bound unto nor what there is excepted out of the said graunt.' [Margl. note: 'The graunt to be produced and lyves to be proved'].

Underwood (if excepted out of the lease) worth £160. [Margl. note: 'These are not excepted.'] Timber trees worth £84. [Margl. note: 'These are excepted.']

Md. 'The present tenant claims these woods by Letters Patent, and upon color there of she sould and fallen parte of the foresaid wood and timber which wee have not valued in the value thereof as aforesaid, but wee esteeme and value the wast thereof to be at £20. [Margl. note: 'This to be considered of.']

[In a different hand] Md. 'that Elizabeth Bligh holds the fifte parte of a certeine peece of arrable land called Crannon Downe conteyninge . . .' 150 ac., worth p.a. £12.

[Margl. note: 'This will appeare when the grant is brought in. Vide the abstract of this grant on the backside of this sheete.']

[m. 3 dorse] The late King by L. P. of 17 April 1628 granted to Mill Bligh, Elizabeth B. his w., and James Cocke three tenements in the occupation of John Hooper in Crannowe [Crannow in St Gennys] and Slade and 2 tenements in Treworgie occupied by John Mill, for their lives. James Cocke is 'onely the life in being now proved'. Entered 29 July 1650.

'FREE-HOLDERS OF THE SAID MANNOR

Thomas French holdeth freely to him and his heires for ever in soccage certeine lands in Canyford [Cansford in Otterham] for which he paieth p.a.' 2s 2d.

John Hooper gent., the same, 1s 10d;   *id.*, the same, 2s;   John Barron sn., moiety of ½ ac. C. in Baskerd [Bastard in St Gennys], John Barron jn., the other moiety, 5s;   James Harrington esq., John Chichester esq., George Lippincott esq., and Richard Hooper, 1 ac. C. in Crosterell, 2s;   *id.*, ½ ac. C. in Manergue, 14s;   James Harrington, John Chichester, George Lippincott, John Arundell de Trerise and George Greenwill kt, 1 ac. C. in Clannow [Crannow in St Gennys], 12s;   Thomas Marten gent., 1½ ac. C. in Penwarne, 8s;   *id.*, 1 ac. C. in Treley [Trelay in St Gennys], 5s;   Digory Poundford esq., heirs of Miles Bligh gent., John Molsworth esq. and Edward Hooper gent., 1 ac. and 1 farl. C. with other lands in Penkevioke [Pencuke], 13s 1d;   Heirs of John Broade gent., Thomas Rowe gent., and John French gent., lands in Maniton, 4s 8d;   John French, 1 farl. in Bandon, 4d;   John Meager and the heirs of John Broade, lands in La Fenn and Maniton, 2s 6d;   Heirs of John Cough gent., mill lands called Fanleston in Warbstowe parish, 2s;   John Hore, mill called Longdowne Mill, near Jacobstowe, 1s 6d;   Heirs of Andrew Rolles esq., the La Woode in St Ginnis, 1s 3d;   The Miller of Tencrucke [Trencreek in St Gennys] Mill pays for a millpool, 4d;   Michael Mayne gent., moiety of lands in Trengeare [Trengayor in St Gennys]; Arthur Asford gent., moiety of the other moiety; Walter Tredennicke gent., the residue, 5s;   John French gent., and John Wood gent. of North Tamerton, lands in Newhame [Newham], 10s; William Cotton clerk and Stephen Marshall, land called La Fenn, 3s 4d; Parishioners of St Gennys for rent of their Church House, 1s.

Total £4 17s 1d.

LEASEHOLDERS

Sir John Walter, Sir James Fullerton, Sir Thomas Trevor, by L. P. of 1628–9,[1] hold in Uphill, 15½ ac. in the occupation of George Copledicke. Term: 31 years. Fine, at the Lord's will. Rent 18s 8d. Impr. val. £8.
Lease assigned 27 March 1628 to Thomas Caldwell esq., who assigned it on 25 Nov. 1630 to Richard Langford, who in turn assigned it 20 March 1631 to George Copledicke, who assigned it on 20 Dec. 1636 to Stephen Bray of St Gennys, yeoman.

The same, in trust and for the use of the late King by L. P. of 14 June 1628, ten. in Uphill, late in the occupation of John More, of 17½ ac. Term: 31 years. Fine, as above. Rent 8s 8d. Impr. val. £8.
Lease assigned 27 March 1628 to Thomas Caldwell, who assigned it 25 Nov. 1630 to Richard Langford, who in turn assigned it 4 March 1631 to William More of St Gennys.

Christopher Bligh claims an estate in a tenement called Trespadocke [Trespaddock in St Gennys] of 30 ac. Term: 31 years. Fine, as above. Rent 4s. Impr. val. £6 6s.
Md. 'That the said Bligh produced not unto us any Letters Pattents, deede, indenture, assignment or other writeing to cleare his estate and title to the last mentioned premisses'. [Margl. note: 'This grant to be produced.']

Thomas Arundell of Trerise esq. claims the moiety of a piece of arable called Crannow Downe but produced neither lease nor L. P., being 75 ac., half of the 150 ac. of the said down. Rent 5s 8d. Impr. val. £28 19s. 4d.
Md. 'the said Mannor lyeth in the parish of St Gynnis and cannot be bounded because it lyeth dispersed into divers parcells, the lands of other lords interveninge'.

CUSTOMS

Two courts leet and two courts baron are held yearly.
Free tenants owe a relief, which with other perquisites amounts on average to 4s 6d.

ABSTRACT

Rents of assize and perquisites	£5 1s 7d
Rents of leasehold lands	£1 7s
Rent of the Barton	£2 12s
Total (sic)	£8 18s 7d
Improved value of the Barton	£110 14s 6d
Improved value of leasehold lands	£51 5s 4d
Total	£161 19s 10d
Woods and underwoods on the Barton	£160
Timber trees and saplings	£84

'This is an exact survey . . .'

[1] Only regnal year given.

52   MANOR OF TYWARNHAYLE

DCO S/5; PRO E 317 (C)/47. This was an ancient manor of the Duchy. It was spread over a large area in Perranzabuloe and neighbouring parishes. It was, along with the manors of Helston and Tewington, one of the chief sources of tin in the Duchy [see No. 16].

'A Survey of the Mannor of Tywarnhayle . . . retorned [10 May 1650],

FREE TENANTS OF THE MANOR

	Fine	Rent
John Sentawbin esq., by the d. of John S. his f.; John Davis gent.; Peter Jenkins gent., by the d. of James Jenkins gent.; John Gregor gent., by the d. of Francis G., and Thomas Arundle esq., by the d. of Thomas A. his f., 1 ac. C. in Lamborne [Lambourne in Perranzabuloe]	1s 4d	9s 8d
John Carter esq., by the d. of Richard C. his bro., 3 parts of 2 ac. C. in Fentengimpes [Ventongimps]; John Cooke, by d. of John C. his f., ¼ of the same	2s	23s 4d
John Cooke esq., by the d. of John C. his f., 8 parts of 9 parts of ⅓ of an ac. C. in Hendragrawen alias Hendraven [Hendrawna in Perranzabuloe]; John Pascoe, ⅑	2s	3s
John Cooke, as above, ½ ac. C. there	nil	4s 9d
Richard Chalenor gent. and John Catcher gent., ⅓ ac. C. there	nil	4s 9d
William Panter esq., by d. of William P. his f., 3 farl. in Hendrokioth	nil	9s 3d
Henry Nance esq., bro. and h. of John N., ½ farl. in Melgessy alias Mevagessy [Menagissey in St Agnes]	nil	3s 1d
Henry Rolle esq., by d. of Dionisius Rolle esq., a 'bedam' mill [*see* p. vi] in Towin [marg. Towyn] [Towan in St Agnes]	nil	6d
John Lord Roberts, by d. of Richard Lord Roberts his f.; John Cooke, as above, and John Chattey gent., by d. of John C. his f., 2 ac. C. in Benathelecke, Callestacke [Callestick], Rees [*id.* in Perranzabuloe] and Bryannecke	1s 4d	nil
Dean and Chapter of the Cathedral of Exeter, 1 landyoke in Kernekeffe [Carnkief]	nil	1s 1½d
Thomas Arundell esq., by d. of Thomas A. his f., moiety of a landyoke in Melenowth	nil	1s 1½d
John Davis, by d. of John D., ⅛; John Sentawbin esq., as above, the residue	nil	1s 1½d
Richard Vivian kt, by d. of Francis V. his f., moiety of a mill in Lameline, alias Veline, alias Melinge	nil	7s 9d
Margarett Rosewarne alias Carlyon, d. and h. of		

	Fine	Rent	
John R. alias C., 2 ac. C. in Bodian, Nanspura and Ruyne	nil	23s	8d
Richard Vivian kt, as above, 1 ac. C. in Pennanns		1s	8d
id., land in Poleglasse		1s	
The Manor of Rillaton 'paieth to this Mannor as quitt rent'		10s	
Total rents of assize		£5 11s	4d

CONVENTIONARY TENANTS OF INHERITANCE

	Fine	Rent	
Thomas Tonkin, by d. of John T. his f., mess. and 12 ac. in Chibundre	2s	10s	4d
id., mess. and 4 ac. in 1 farl. in Chinall	nil	5s	
Honor Gregor wid., by d. of Francis G. gent. her hbd., 2 parts of a mess. and 9 ac. in 3 farl. in Trewicke	nil	6s	8d
id., 11 ac. in Trewicke		6s	
John Bennett and Christian his w. in her own right, moiety of mess. and 7 ac. in Trewicke; Ralphe Tudd, the other moiety	2s	6s	8d
Honor Gregor, as above, ⅓ of a mess. and 14 ac. in Trewicke; Sampson Michell, the residue	nil	13s	10d
Peran Hoskin, by surr. of Francis Gregor, mess. and 6 ac. in 1 farl. there	1s	1s	
John Michell, by surr. of Thomas Coath, mess. and ¼ mess. and 9 ac. in Trewicke	nil	3s	
id., as above, mess. and ⅓ mess. there		8s	8d
John Gregor, in right of Anne his w., mess. and 7 ac. there		8s	8d
Another mess. and 21 ac. which all the tenants of the manor took at the last Assession because the tenant had left it in the Lord's hand, since the Manor is liable to make good the rent		8s	
Sampson Michell, in his own right, ⅓ of 3 mess. and 13 ac. in Trewicke; William Lanyon, the residue	nil	13s	2d
John Bennett, in right of Christian his w., by surr. of Benedict B., moiety of 2 mess. and 11 ac.; Ralphe Tudd, in his own right, the other moiety	nil	12s	4d
Edward Cottie, by surr. of Ralphe Edge, 2 mess. and 35 ac. in 1 farl. in Scavengroves	6s	6s	
John Crocker gent., mess. and 38 ac. and 1½ rods and also ⅓ mess. and 28½ ac., previously Thomas Hoster's; another mess. and 28 ac. 1½ rods; ⅓ mess. and 38½ ac. previously John Jagowe's; another mess. and 38 ac. 1½ rods, part of 4 mess., previously Ewringe's; all in Trenelles	8s 11d	46s	8d
Margarett Chatcher, by d. of William Catcher her hbd., mess. and 5 ac. in Ponslusson	2d	7s	4d
id., as above, mess. and 3 ac. in Tywarnailewartha [Tywarnhayle]	nil	4s	

	Fine	Rent
id., as above, mess. and 12 ac. in Tregondy	2s	1s
William Nicholas, by d. of Aurick N., mill called Tywarnaile alias Trewarnethicke Mill	8s 4d	8s 4d
Honor Gregor, as above, $\frac{1}{6}$ of the pasture in Pennans; John Bennett, in right of Christian his w., $\frac{1}{12}$; Perran Hoskin, by surr. of Francis Gregor, $\frac{1}{6}$; John Michell, by surr. of Thomas Coath, $\frac{1}{6}$; John Gregor, in right of Anne his w., $\frac{1}{6}$; Sampson Michell and William Lanyon, $\frac{1}{6}$; Sampson Richards, in right of Grace his w., by d. of Ralphe Barrett, the residue	nil	3s
Grace Pendarves, by d. of Samuell P. her hbd., pasture of Goen Enis alias Rosemundy [Gooninis and Rosemundy in St Agnes] of 20 ac.	nil	1s
John Pawle, moiety of a moiety of mess. and 10 ac. in $\frac{1}{3}$ ac. C. in Trevissacke alias Trevisacke [Trevissick in St Agnes]; John Cleather, by surr. of Richard Danyell, the other moiety of the said moiety	4s	4s
id., moiety of a moiety of mess. and 10 ac. there; John Cleather, as above, the other moiety	4s	4s
id., moiety of mess. and 19 ac. in Trevisacke; John Cleath, as above, the other moiety	4s	4s
id., moiety of mess. and 19 ac. there; John Cleather, as above, the other moiety	nil	9s 6d
id., in right of Thomasin his w., 2 mess. and 17 ac. in 3 farl. in Trevissacke	8s 4d	8s 4d
id., as above, 2 mess. and 17 ac. in 3 farl. there	nil	8s 4d
Henry Edmonds gent., by surr. of John Kent, $\frac{1}{3}$ part and a moiety of another third of mess. and 24 ac. in Bans [Banns in St Agnes] 'except a mill called a stamping mill'; Thomas Martyn, by surr. of John Tregea, the said mill; William Tregea, by surr. of John T. and Richard Treall, by surr. of John Tonkin, the residue	3s 4d	12s 2d
William Tregea, $\frac{1}{3}$ of a pasture in Bans; Thomas Martyn, by surr. of said William T., the residue	nil	6d
William Nicholas, by d. of Aurich N. his m., 1 ac. with a corn mill built thereon in Tavisecke and Bans	3s	2s
Christopher Colmer, by marr. of Ursula C. his m., moiety of 40 ac. in 1 farl. in Polgoda [*id.* in Perranzabuloe]; Anne Cooke wid. by d. of John C. her hbd., the other moiety	3s 8d	3s 8d
Sampson Michell, $\frac{1}{3}$ of a landyoke called Talreyn; the tenants of Trevithecke, the residue	nil	2s 6d
id., $\frac{1}{3}$ of 6 parts of a landyoke called Rualyn; the tenants of Trevithecke, the residue	nil	5s 4d

	Fine	Rent
Thomas Tonkin, by d. of John T., a landyoke called Goenfree	2s	2s
There is a pasture called Polglasse, lately held by Anne Davis, but now no tenant; formerly paid	nil	1s 8d
Anne Cooke wid., by d. of John C. her hbd., piece of waste in Engilly [Engelly in Perranzabuloe]	2s	1s
Thomas Tonkin, by d. of John T., pasture of Presincoll of 20½ ac.	7s	3s 6d
id., as above, a landyoke in Presincoll, being 20½ ac. of waste	7s	3s 6d
Sampson Michell, ⅛ of a third and ⅙ of one landyoke in Reserffe; tenants of Trevethicke, residue	nil	1s
John Crocker gent., the pinfold of Tywarnhaile	nil	6d
John Michell, 'to and for the use of the tennants of Tywarnhaile', the 'adiustment' [agistment] of Goensatha, Donsatha and Donhaver [Goonhavern]	nil	2s
Thomas Pawle, moiety of 1 ac. of waste in Trevisicke; Symon Pawle, by d. of Barrucke Paule the other moiety	nil	2s
Joan Cooke wid., by d. of Edward C. her hbd, 6 ac. of waste in Goenbrey [Goonvrea in St Agnes] and 'a certeine house called Stowe Mill with a knocking mill there'.	nil	1s
Thomas Pawle, ½ ac. of waste 'in the moores of Trevisecke on which is built a stampinge mill for the cleanseing of tinn'	nil	1s
Henry Nance esq., 'a quarry of stone in Gole Trevennis upon condicon that if the rent thereof shalbe behinde and unpaide he shall forfeite to the Lord of the Mannor all his other lands within the said Mannor and also that the Reeve of the Mannor may (when the rent shalbe unpaide) distreyne on all his lands and tenements	nil	1s
There is one mill called a stampinge mill late held by Anne Davis wid. by d. of Robert D. her hbd., 'but since his decease there hath noe tennant taken the same'		2s
Henry Nance esq., 'a certeine little isle called Bond'		1s
Thomas Michell, by surr. of John M., 'a certeine course of water runninge to a fullinge mill'		6d
Thomas Tonkin, 2 'bedam' mills [*see* p. vi] in Goen Enys [Gooninis in St Agnes]		1s

TENANTS AT THE WILL OF THE LORD[1]

Anne Davis wid. (dec.) held 'a certeine chappell within the parish of Perran in Zabulo by vertue of a graunt from the commissioneers of the last Assession' for 7 years only; now in the lord's hand. Rent 1s.

[1] Tenants at will were very rare on the ancient manors of the Duchy.

Margarett Catcher wid., by d. of William C. her hbd., third of the waste called Tywarnhayle Downe, alias Cloyder Downe, of 40 ac.; John Crocker gent., the residue. Fine 4s. Rent 2s.

Thomas Tonkin, 2 mills called the Upper Stampinge Mill and the Nether Stamping Mill, built without licence on the Lord's common of Chivander and Portrevanance [Trevaunance Cove]. Fine nil. Rent 10s.

John Polwheele, royalties of the manor. Fine 6d. Rent 1s.

'All which are worth at an improved value'   £3 10s.

Md. 'that the value of the Tolle Tynn . . . is alsoe certified in grosse with the lease thereof herewith retorned that the last Assessions for this mannor was held [9 Sept. 1645]'

[BOUNDS]

The Mannor 'cannot be bounded in regard it lieth devided into divers places and severall partes thereof lie distinct and severed each from other by the lords of divers lands which cannot be particulerly expressed.'

[COMMONS]

The commons are 'taken by tennants . . . as is expressed in theire severall holdings before recited.'

CUSTOMS OF THE MANOR

A court leet is held twice yearly and a court baron every three weeks.
The Assessions Court meets every seven years. New knowledge money amounts on average to 10s yearly. Fines are paid over the following six years.
Freeholders pay a relief and customary tenants a heriot.
Customary tenants are to serve as reeve, tithing man, beadle and 'viewer of reparacions'.
Widows may hold their husbands' tenements during their widowhood.

Md. 'That the Deputy Admirall Mr Porter hath encroached on the custome of this Mannor by takeing away a certeine wreacke which was taken up within this Mannor by the reeve thereof about the 29th December last and was valued to be worth 20s'.

ABSTRACT

Rents of assize with tin fines and perquisites	£10 11s 4d
Rents of conventionary tenants and of tenants at will	£14 2s 2d
Old knowledge money, on average	12s 5¾d and ⅐ of ¾d.
New knowledge money, on average	10s
Total	£25 15s 11¾d and ⅐ of ¾d.

Improved value of tenements held by tenants at will £3 10s

'This is an exact survey . . . [sd]'

53   MANOR OF WEST ANTHONY

DCO S/4; PRO E 317 (C)/54. This small manor consisted of scattered parcels in the adjoining parishes of Antony, St John Rame and Sheviock. It came to the Duchy as part of the lands of Henry Courtenay, Marquis of Exeter.

'A Survey of the Mannor of West Anthony . . . retorned [12 February 1649/50].

FREE-HOLDERS

Sir Samuell Rolles, Francis Fortescue esquire and Thomas Furlong Gentleman hold freely to them and theire heires for ever certeine lands in Carbeele in fee simple or fee tayle, for which they pay to the Lord' p.a. 1s.

Richard Carew esq., lands in East Anthony	2s
Nicholas Bettersby gent., lands in Rame [*id.*]	1s
Simon Rowe, gent., lands in Somwill, 'a garland of red honeysuckles'	
John Elliott, lands in St Johns [St John]	4d
Francis Wills esq., lands in Little Wolsden [Wolsdon]	5s
Henry Rolles esq., lands in Hill	5s
Heirs of Sir Warwicke Heale, lands in St Johns	4d
Philip Blacke, lands in St Johns	2d
Heirs of Thomas Searle gent., lands in St Johns	2d
id., lands in Pengelley	4s 8d
John Harris esq., John Clobery and Christopher Ough gent., lands in Penhergett	1s 11d
John Lawndrie, lands in Combe Parke	10d
Total	£1 2s 3d

COPYHOLDERS

Ferdinando Trigg (40), s. of John T.; Walter T. (dec.) s. of Walter T., and George T. (25) s. of William T., by copy of 28 Sept. 1630, mess. and ten. called Crasdon of 36 ac. with half of wood called Brockhole Woode. Term: lives successively. Rent 14s 4d. Impr. val. £17 12s 6d.

John Trigg (dec.), Margarett (dec.) his w. and John T. (35) their s., by copy of 28 Sept. 1630, mess. in Brockhole, except a moiety of Brockhole Woode of 37 ac. Term: lives successively. Fine, at the Lord's will. Rent 14s 4d. Impr. val. £21.

Anthony Furlong gent. (60) and Richard F. (dec.), by copy of 17 Aug. 1612, ten. in West Anthony of 66 ac. Term: lives successively. Fine, as above. Rent 20s 5½d. Impr. val. £44.
Reversion granted 7 Feb. 1638 to Gonepert Furlong wid. (36) and John F. (16) her s.

Elizabeth Lugger (dec.), Walter L. (dec.) and Joan (60) his w., by copy of 17 Aug. 1612, ten. in Trewalla [?Trevol] of 43 ac. Term: lives successively. Fine, as above. Rent 13s 6½d. Impr. val. £22 1s 5½d.
Joan Luggar is now Joan Stockman. Reversion granted 12 April 1640 to William Lugger (35) and Alice (28) his w. for their lives.

Joan Poplestone wid. (44), by copy of 24 Sept. 1622, ten. of 33 ac. in Combe [Coombe]. Term, life. Fine, as above. Rent 6s 8d. Impr. val. £19.

James Ede (36), by copy of 25 Sept. 1628, ten. in Trevalla of 21 ac. Term: life. Fine, as above. Rent 6s 9¾d and half a farthing. Impr. val. £12 4s.

James Ede (36), Marie (33) his w., and Mary (8) their d., by copy of 29 July 1642, ten. in Trevalla, previously in possession of Simon Row, of 16 ac. Term: lives successively. Fine, as above. Rent 6s 9¾d and half a farthing. Impr. val. £9 19s.

Joan Rewe wid. (70), Robert R. (34) her s., by copy of 28 Sept. 1614, ten. in Trevalla of 40 ac. Term: lives successively. Fine, as above. Rent 13s 6¾d. Impr. val. £24 10s.

Thomasin Brusy wid. (60) and John B. (40) her s. and Simea (dec.) his w., by copy of 28 Sept. 1630, ten. in Trevalla of 38 ac. Term: lives successively. Fine, as above. Rent 13s 6¾d. Impr. val. £20 9s.
Reversion granted 18 Feb. 1641 to Mary Brusey (36) now w. of John B. for life.

Thomas Nelder (30) and Joan (28) his w., by copy of 4 May 1642; ten. in Eastley of 40 ac. Term: lives successively. Fine, as above. Rent 28s. Impr. val. £26 5s.

Henrie Hancocke and Walter H., by copy of 4 March 1631, moiety of ten. in Pengelley of 36 ac. Term: lives successively. Fine, as above. Rent 10s 4d. Impr. val. £19 5s.

Ede Reape w. of John R., by copy of 17 Aug. [—],[1] ten. in Le Hay [Hay] of 59 ac. Term: life. Fine, as above. Rent 24s. Impr. val. £34 7s 6d.
Reversion granted 17 June, 1628 to John Reape (69) hbd. of Ede R. and Ferdinando (28 their s. Term: lives.

William Wilshman (64) and Elizabeth (52) his w., by copy of 28 July 1614, ten. of 65 ac. in West Anthony. Fine, as above. Rent £1 0s 5½d. Worth £46.
Reversion granted 28 Sept. 1630 to William W. (28) their son.

Robert Hendy (70), by copy of 22 Sept. 1587, ten. in West Anthony of 64 ac. Fine, as above. Rent 20s 5½d. Impr. val. £43 10s.
Reversion granted 17 Aug. 1612 to Elizabeth Hendy (64) w. of Robert H. and Thomas (44) their s.

Richard Carew esq. (dec.), Alexander C. gent. (dec.) and John C. gent. (28), sons of Richard C., by copy of 28 Sept. 1630, the fishing of the water called Thankes Bay, Pengelley Bay and one half of the fishing of St Peters Bay, St Johns Bay and Makerslake. Term: lives successively. Fine, as above. Rent 2s 8d. Impr. val. 28s.

Mary Leman (30) w. of Peter L., Peter L. (9) and John L. (8) their sons, by copy of 20 July 1634, piece of land called Millhill of ¼ ac. Term: lives successively. Fine, as above. Rent 1s 4d. Impr. val. 12s.

Richard Rundle (50) and Mary R. (50) his w., by copy of 9 Aug. 1622, ten. in West Anthony of 67 ac. Term: lives successively. Fine, as above. Rent 20s 9½d. Impr. val. £44 12s 3d.

Walter Deble (40), Agnes (38) his w. and John (7) their s., copy not

[1] No regnal year given.

produced, ten. in Hole of 37 ac. Term: lives successively. Fine, as above. Rent 13s 4d. Impr. val. £20 10s.

Grace Milner (60) and Richard M. (40) claim to hold by copy a moiety of a ten. in Pengelly of 36 ac. Term: lives successively. Fine, as above. Rent 10s. Impr. val. £15.

Baronett Carew (15) and Mary C. (13) his s., [sic] ten. called Weareland [Wareland] of 12 ac. which is intermixed with the Barton of East Anthony and other lands of Baronet Carew. Term: live successively. Fine, as above. Rent 8s. Impr. val. £5 12s.

BOUNDS
'The said Mannor of West Anthony is bounded as followeth: by the lands of Barronett Carew on the Northwest, North and east sides; by the lands of Mr Searle on the southeast; by the lands of Judge Rolle on the south; by the lands of Symon Row on the southwest, and by the lands of Mr Robert Skawen on the west.'

CUSTOMS
Two courts leet and two courts baron are held yearly.
Relief and heriot are payable on death of the tenant or alienation or surrender of the tenement.
Three tenements, namely Eastley, Crasdon and Hole are to provide a reeve. In the case of copyhold tenements by inheritance the executors of the last life are to hold the tenement until the Michaelmas following.

ABSTRACT[2]

Rents of assize and perquisites	£5 2s 3d
Rents of copyhold tenants	£13 16s 7¾d
	Total £18 18s 10¾d
Improved value of copyhold land	£448 12s 8½d

'This is an Exact Survey . . .'

54 MANOR OF BRADFORD, DEVON

DCO S/4; PRO E 317 (D)/17. The manor lay in several parcels scattered over the parishes of Pyworthy and Clawton. It belonged to the Priory of St Stephen, Launceston, and came to the Duchy in 1540.

'A Survey of the Mannor of Bradford . . . in the County of Devon . . . retorned [7 June 1650].

FREE-TENNANTS OF THE SAID MANNOR
Sir Nicholas Martyn holdeth freely to him and his heires for ever in soccage the moiety of one tenement called Marsh', paying yearly 1s 6d.

Henry Walter gent., lands called Winscott	10s
Heirs of Mr Nowcott, lands in Winscott	2s 8d
Total rents of assize	14s 2d

[2] The last membrane, containing the Abstract, is missing from the Duchy copy of the Survey.

LEASEHOLDERS OF THE MANOR

Henry Wolrond, by L. P. of 25 Feb. 1628, ten. called Horslade alias Hogslayde [Horslett] in Clawton Parish, Devon, late part of the possessions of the Prior of Launceston and now annexed to the Dukedom of Cornwall, together with a mess., a barn, 2 gardens, 4 orchards, a 'hophaie', a dove house and 145½ ac. of meadow and pasture, namely: a close of 35 ac. called Horslade Lea, a close of 2¼ ac. and 28 perches called East Culver Close, a close of 2½ ac. and 14 perches called West Culver Close, a close of 2¾ ac. and 10 perches called South East Parke alias Will Parke, a close of 2½ ac. and 13 perches called Wester South Parke, a close of 6¼ ac. and 13 perches called South Broade Close, North Broade Close of 7 ac. and 29 perches, East Broad Close of 2 ac. 23 perches, Little Furse Close of 2¼ ac. and 37 perches, Horslade Comons of 33 ac. 20 perches, the Great Haim of 17 ac., 2 closes called the Little Hamms of 13¾ ac. 14 perches, Bremble Parke of 1¼ ac. and 10 perches, the Will Parke of 3½ ac. Term: 99 years, on lives of John Arscott (30), William Arscotte (26) and Anne (28), children of Edward Arscott of Tettcott [Tetcott], Devon. Rent £2. Heriot £1 10s. Fine at the lord's will. Impr. val. £66 13s.

Exceptions, etc.: to maintain the premises 'in good and sufficient repair'; sufficient timber allowed 'by the appointment of the Steward and not otherwise'; to plant 6 trees yearly. Sufficient boots allowed.

Trees and saplings now growing are worth £12 10s.

John Pearce, by L. P. of 31 Oct. 1627, mess., land and ten. in Pinkeworthy the Higher and Pinkeworthy the Nether [Pinkworthy] in Pyeworthy [Pyworthy] Parish, Devon, with 'one mill for corne and one fulling mill in Pinkeworthy the Neather'; in all 64 ac., with 'leates, waters, watercourses, suites to the mill, fludgates, headeweares'. Term: 99 years on lives of J. P. (50), Penelope (40) his w., and Mary Corie (24), d. of William Corie of Pieworthy. Rent £1 16s 1½d. Heriot £1 10s. Fine, as above. Impr. val. £19 10s.

Exceptions, etc.; to plant 4 trees yearly.

Richard Sheere, by L. P. of 15 Feb. 1628, moiety of ten. in Pinckworthy of 40 ac. Term: 99 years on lives of Alice (6), w. of R. S., Samuel (dec.) and William Sheare (dec.) their sons; Samuell 'was kild in the service of the Parlyament'. Rent 16s. Heriot 10s. Fine, as above. Impr. val. £15.

Exceptions, etc.; to plant 3 trees yearly, Alice S. is in possession.

Richard Cornew, by L. P. of 25 Feb. 1628, 'all those messuages, lands and tenements called Bradford' [in Pyworthy], in all 44 ac. Term: 99 years, on lives of R. C. (36), and Leonard C. (28) and Hannah C. (27), his children. Rent 18s. Heriot £1. Impr. val. £21 4s. Fine, as above.

Exceptions, etc.; to plant 4 trees yearly.

John Frayne de Langtree, by lease of 3 Dec. 1622, ten. called Bradford in Pyworthy parish 'and one messuage or mansion house, one barne, one sheephouse, one stable, one garden, two orchards and halfe of the Towne-place', in all 1¼ ac. and 10 roods, and also 63¾ ac. 24 roods of land, meadow and pasture, namely: the closes called Higher East Parke of 3¼ ac. and 15 roods; Lower East Parke of 2 ac. and 27 roods; Higher Above Towne of 2 ac. 7 roods; Lower Above Towne of 2¾ ac. 25 roods; South Parke of 4¾ ac. 2

roods; Shortland of 2¼ ac. 27 roods; Highermoore of 4¾ ac.; the Lower Moore of 10½ ac. 33 roods; the Hamme 'in the lower parte of the Lower Moore' of 5 ac. 10 roods; South Hamme of 7 ac. 20 roods; the Furse Close of 1¼ ac. 4 roods; two closes called the Langlands of 7 ac. 34 roods; a piece of land in Marshmeade alias Broade Meadow of 1½ ac. 6 roods; a close called the Parke above Waste of 1¼ ac. 4 roods. Term: 99 years on lives of Grace (53) w. of J. F., and Thomas (32) and Robert (22) his sons. Rent 18s. Heriot £4. Fine, as above. Impr. val. £34 11s 6d. Exceptions, etc.; to plant 7 trees yearly.

'This Mannor of Bradford is not to be bounded for that the tenements thereof lye in two parishes, viz. the parish of Pieworthy and the parish of Clawton, and are distincte severed the one from the other by the lands of other lords'.

CUSTOMS OF THE MANOR
A Court Leet should be held twice yearly, and at the Michaelmas court a Reeve should be chosen to collect the Lord's rents, and also reliefs, heriots, fines and other casualties.
Free tenents pay a relief on every death or alienation; leasehold tenants pay a heriot.

AN ABSTRACT OF THE PRESENT RENTS AND FUTURE IMPROVEMENTS WITH OTHER PROFITS OF THE MANOR

Rents of assize and perquisites	£1 2s 2d
Rents of tenements in lease	£6 8s 1½d
Total	£7 10s 3½d
Improved value of the tenements held in lease after the expiry of the present leases, beside the present rent	£156 18s 6d
Timber trees are worth	£12 10s

'This is an exact survey . . . [sd]

55 HONOUR, MANOR AND BOROUGH OF BRADNINCH, DEVON

DCO S/8; PRO E 317 E (D)/5 and 6. The Public Record Office has two copies of the Survey. The manor lay mainly in the parish of Bradninch, but included as its *caput* Rougemont Castle in Exeter. It ranked as one of the *forinseca maneria* of the Duchy, and had been part of the Duchy from its inception.

'A Survey of the Honor, Mannor and Burroughe of Bradninch . . . retorned [20 Nov. 1650].

'THE MANNOR OR MANSION HOUSE
The said house is knowen by the name of the Castle of Exeter and is scituate within the walls of the City of Exeter, is in reasonable good repair, the houses therein being lately repaired by the present Governor whoe keepes a garison therein for the Parliament. The which Castle with the ditches thereto belonging were worth in the yeare 1640 [£30 p.a.] the said ditches

being then converted into gardens and sett with fruite trees, but since the said Castle was garrisoned the foresaid gardens have been layed wast, soe that the scite of the Castle at present is worth [13s 4d p.a.]. But the said Castle being garrisoned and not to be sould, we value the ditches besides the Castle to be worth upon improvement p.a. £5.

'There are alsoe adjoyning to the said Castle six severall tenements in very good repaire with gardens unto them belonging, now in the occupacion of severall under tennants, which are worth upon improvement' p.a. £2 15s.

These premises are let by lease from the late King, when Prince of Wales and Duke of Cornwall, of 22 Jan. 1619 to John Mules gent. for 99 years on the lives of Phillip Bigleston, John B. and Thomas B.,[1] paying £1 5s p.a. and 12s as a heriot.

Exceptions: all lands, rents and profits in Crockerne Well, Dorscombe and Buglebrooke, all of them in Devon, in any way belonging to the Castle. Also 'all tenths, advowsons, knights' fees, wards, relieffes to the said Castle apperteyninge. And all great trees, woodes, underwoodes . . .'

Lessee to keep premisses in good repair.

'The relict of Phillip Bigglestone deceased, whoe had the same assigned unto him by the foresaid Mules is in present possession of the premisses. The other two lives are reputed to be liveinge, they being both beyond the seas and not heard from these twelve moneths.'

Free tenants of the Manor

Henry Earle of Bath, in knight service, Manor of Combyntynheade [Combeinteignhead], 'but by what number or parte of knights fees he holdeth the same is not certeine'.

Symon Leach esq. in knight service, manor of Cadley [Cadeleigh] by 1 knight's fee.

Sir John Chichester bart., manors of Buckland Denham [North Buckland] in the parish of Georgeham, being 3 parts of a knight's fee.

id., manors of Huggeston [Haxton] and benton [*id.*] in the parish of Bratton Fleminge [Bratton Fleming] for 1 kn. fee.

Heirs of Dillon, lands in the parish [sic] of Buckland Denham for ¼ kn. fee.

John Smyth esq., moiety of the manor of Ivedon [*id.*] in the parish of Owliscombe [Awliscombe] for one part of ½ kn. fee.

Sir Thomas Mallett, the other moiety, for like part of knight's fee.

Heirs of Cottle, mess. or ten. called Buckland Denham in Georgeham parish, for a moiety of 3 parts of a kn. fee.

Sir Francis Fulford kt, mess. or ten. called Godford in Owliscombe [Awliscombe], for ⅛ of a kn. fee.

[—] Pyne esq., manor of Withangers [Woolhanger] in the parish of Lynton, for ¼ kn. fee.

Heirs of Bellew, lands in Esse alias Aish Roades [Ash] in Braunton parish, for ½ kn. fee.

[1] No ages given.

Heirs of Huckmoore, manor of Buckland Baron [Buckland] in Combyn-tynhead [Combeinteignhead] parish, for 1 kn. fee.

id., manor of Netherton [*id.*] in the same parish, for 1 kn. fee.

Heirs of Chichester, manor of Wollacombe Tracy [Wollacombe] in the parish of Morthowe [Morthoe], for $\frac{1}{4}$ kn. fee.

Heirs of Gifford, manor of Buckland Chelowe [?Buckland in parish of Braunton] for 1 kn. fee.

Heirs of William Walrond esq., lands in Wonford St Loy [Wonford] in Hevitree [Heavitree] parish and in Leymore [Moor] in Sowton [*id.*] for $\frac{1}{4}$ kn. fee.

Arthur Upton, manor of Farrwoode [Fairwood] in the parish of St Mary Tedburne [Tedburn St Mary], for $\frac{1}{2}$ kn. fee.

Heirs of Robert Davie, manor of Combelancy [Combelancey] in Sandford (*id.*) parish, for $\frac{1}{4}$ kn. fee.

Heirs of [—] Berry esq., manor of Eastley [Eastleigh] in the parish of Westley [Westleigh], for 1 kn. fee.

Henry Cruys, manor of Cruysmorchard [Cruwys Morchard] in the parish of Cruysmorchard, for 1 kn. fee.

Heirs of John Wood gent., lands in Buckland Denham [North Buckland] in Georgeham parish, for a moiety of 3 parts of a kn. fee.

Heirs of William Hord, manor of East Memburie in the parish of Memburie [Membury], for 1 kn. fee.

[—] Sydenham esq., manor of South Radworthie [South Radworthy] in the parish of North Molton (*id.*), for $\frac{1}{3}$ kn. fee.

[—] Cuckfield esq., moiety of Cottersey [Cottarson] in Owliscombe [Awliscombe], for $\frac{1}{8}$ kn. fee.

id., lands in Owliscombe [Awliscombe] called Weppringston [Waringston] for $\frac{1}{4}$ kn. fee.

Heirs of [—] Jesse, $\frac{1}{6}$ of Cottersey [Cottarson in Awliscombe] for $\frac{1}{6}$ kn. fee.

[—] Champneys esq., $\frac{1}{4}$ of Cottersey for $\frac{1}{4}$ kn. fee.

William Glandvile, $\frac{1}{4}$ of ten. and 40 ac. called Leemoore [Moor] in the parishes of Sowton and Heavitree, for $\frac{1}{4}$ kn. fee.

Heirs of Mortimoore alias Tanner, lands and tens. in Bradford Tracie [Bradford] in Witheridge (*id.*) parish, for $\frac{1}{2}$ kn. fee.

Samuel Mortimoore alias Tanner, lands and tens. in Bradford, called Berdon, in Witheridge parish, 'by what parte of a knights fee wee can not fynde'.

Heirs of [—] Loveringe, lands and tens. called Furshill [Furzehill] in Lynton parish, for $\frac{1}{20}$ kn. fee.

id., land called Radsprey [Ratsbury] and Spreyhanger [Sparhanger] in the village of Hillerington [Ilkerton] in Lynton parish, for $\frac{1}{4}$ kn. fee.

Heirs of [—] Hayes, 5 parts in 6 of the manor of Puddington [*id.*], for $\frac{5}{6}$ of $\frac{1}{2}$ kn. fee.

Heirs of Hugh Hayes, $\frac{1}{6}$ of the manor of Puddington, for $\frac{1}{12}$ kn. fee.

Heirs of Fish, lands and tens. in Leemoore [Moor] in Sowton par. and St Loy and Wendford [Wonford] in Heavitree par., for $\frac{1}{4}$ kn. fee.

Heirs of Blackaller, ten. and 40 ac. of land and 30 ac. of pasture 10 ac. of meadow and 10 ac. of furse and heath in Swymbridge [Swimbridge], 'but by what parte of a knights fee is not certeine'.

Heirs of Saunders, ten. in Swymbridge, part of the Manor of Stoford, as above.

Roger Leighe, $\frac{1}{4}$ of a ten. and 66 ac. in Leemore in Sowton par., for $\frac{1}{4}$ kn. fee; and $\frac{1}{4}$ of a ten. and $\frac{1}{4}$ of a piece of land in Sowton, in the manor of Wondford [Wonford], for $\frac{1}{20}$ kn. fee.

Heirs of Thomas Melhuish, moiety of ten. and 50 ac. of land called Combe [Coombe] in Puddington par., for $\frac{1}{4}$ kn. fee.

Md. 'that there is yearely collected by Thomas Gewen esq., feodary and escheator of the Dukedom of Cornewall, certeine escheated rents paid by severall persons within the County of Devon and belonging to this Honor of Bradninch, but how much it is, or by whom paid wee are not certeine, the said Gewen haveing not produced unto us by what graunt he holds the said places nor anything at all concerninge the said rents.'

Reliefs within the Honour are leased, together with the Honors of Launceston and Trematon, to Rebecca Birde at a yearly rent of £8 4s 2d, but R. B. did not produce the lease, 'the improvement of which relieffes (if continued to be paid) we value to be worth (besides the rent paid by the said Bird) for this Mannor' p.a. £6 13s 4d.
The freeholders also pay £1 10s which is collected by the Bailiff for respite of homage.

COPYHOLDERS OF THE BARTON LANDS WITHIN THE MANOR
John Wright jn. (30), Peter W. (30) and William W. (27), children of John W. of Bowell sn., by copy of 17 April 1622, 'the vesture or sheere of one acre of meadow in Longmeade', part of the Barton lands, for their lives. Rent 4s 6d. Impr. val. 18s.

Samuel Sainthill (22), Grace S. (dec.) and Vreth S. (dec.) children of Peter S. esq., by copy of 7 dec. 1628, 'vesture and sheere' of the eighth and ninth acres of the Greate Meadow called Longmeade, for lives. Rent 8s. Impr. val. £1 16s.

Thomasin Denner (dec.), w. of John Denner, John (32) their s. and Thomas Harecourte (dec.) jn., by copy of 27 March 1617, 6 closes, 4 of which are called Parkeland alias Cholwill Cleeves, another called Cholwill Moore and the other, Burhaye, containing in all 10 ac., for lives. Rent 14s 6d. Impr. val. £9.

John Denner sn. (dec.), Thomasin (dec.), his w. and John (32) their s., by copy of the above date, land called Marshes, of 26 ac. for lives. Rent £1 0s 8d. Impr. val. £24.

The same, by copy of the same date, 4 closes of land and pasture called Marshes and also 3 other closes called the Seven Acres, containing altogether 19 ac. Rent £1 12s. Impr. val. £23.
The reversion of the last granted 31 July 1622 to Alexander Denner (28) and Judith D. (30) children of J. D., for lives. Rent, as above.

Thomasin Denner (dec.), w. of John D. sn., and John (32) their s. and Thomas Hartcourte jn. (dec.), by copy of 27 March 1617, vesture and 'cuttage' of 2 ac. and 1 rood of meadow 'lying in the east parte of the Greate Meadow called the Long Meadow', for lives. Rent 8s. Impr. val. £2.

Thomasin Denner and John D. (32) her s., as above, piece of land called Downe of 76 ac. for lives. Rent 14s. Impr. val. £23.

The timber trees, pollards and saplings growing on the foresaid tens. to the number of 20 are worth £5.

John Holwill (40) and Thomas H. (30), sons of Grace H., by copy of 1 Oct. 1627, ten. and 4 closes called Westbeare and Cholwill Moore, containing 8 ac., for lives. Rent 12s. Impr. val. £5 9s.

John Forse (60), Alexander (23) his s., and Johan (30) and Elenor (35) his ds. [no date], 4 ac. and 1 rood called Middlemeade and a close called West Feild of 4 ac., for lives. Rent £1 1s 6d. Impr. val. £7 8s 6d.

Thomasin Torre (dec.), Agnes T. (dec.) and Barbara T. (60), ds. of George T., by copy of [. . .] March 1593 parcell called the Pinfold containing 10½ ac., for lives. Rent 5s 10d. Impr. val. £7.

Henry Saunders (dec.), Elizabeth (50) his w. and Michael (20) their s., by copy of 13 April 1637, for lives, 10 ac. of Barton land. Rent 5s 10d. Impr. val. £7.

Joan Mortimore (dec.), Thomas M. (68) and Elizabeth M. (21), by copy of 21 Dec. 1624, 'mill called a fullinge mill and 7 acres of Barton land thereunto belonging', for lives. Rent £1 3s 1d. Impr. val. £7 7s.

Willmot Wright (dec.) w. of John W. jn., Margery (30) their d. and Ann (dec.) sister of John, by copy of 28 July 1613, parcel of Barton land called Foxenhole of 4½ ac., for lives. Rent 9s. Impr. val. £4.
The reversion is said to have been granted to John Wright (30) for life, but the copy was not produced. Rent, as above.

John Harcourte (dec.), Elizabeth H. (38) and Hellen H. (30) children of Thomas H., by copy of 17 Dec. 1633, 4 closes called Barton Downes containing 13¼ ac., for lives. Rent 7s 10d. Impr. val. £9.

The same, by copy of the same date, 'the sheere or cutting' of 1 ac. of meadow in the Great Meadow, for lives. Rent 4s. Impr. val. 18s.

Edward Mortimore (dec.), William M. (dec.) and Thomas M. (68), by copy of 27 Feb. 1595, 4 closes called Parkeland containing 11 ac. for lives. Rent 7s 5d. Impr. val. £9 3s.

Reversion granted 11 Oct. 1638 to Mary (16) and Elizabeth (21), children of Thomas M. Rent, as above.

Robert Taylor (55), Peter T. (27) and Elinor T. (30), by copy of 26 Oct. 1620, 2 closes called Cholwillmoore and Trymline Parke, containing 4 ac., with 'sheere of one acre of meadow in Longe Meade', for lives. Rent 8s for closes; 4s for the 'sheere'. Worth £5 10s.

Robert Taylor, Peter T. and Elionor T., as above, a moore called Cholwillmoore of 1½ ac. Rent 8s. Worth £2.

Peter Taylor and Elionor T. children of Robert T., by copy of 10 April 1634, mess. and 4 ac., part of the Barton of Bradninch, for lives. Rent 7s. Worth £3. Both lives in being.

Thomas Roades (dec.) and Mary R. (60), by copy of 30 March 1609, ten. called Westbeare and Cholwichmoore 'as it is devided, viz. all those two closes of land called the Drie Close [4 ac.] that Moore [3 roods] one orchard adjoyninge to the said Moore [1 rood], one meadow called the Little Meade [1 ac.] and one house called Tannehouse', for lives. Rent 8s. Worth £5 4s. The reversion granted 5 Dec. 1619 to Thomas Roades (30), Willmott (35) and Sith R. (28) for lives.

Dorothie Sainthill wid. (50), Mary S. (28) and Samuell S. (23) gent., by copy of 19 Dec. 1627, 'corn mills called Kensam Mills with a course of water and suit of multure of the tenants and alsoe divers parcels of land called Millhams, Okehams and Long Millway', containing 16 ac. of meadow and pasture, for lives. Rent of mills £4 13s 4d; of land £1 4s 2d. Worth £110.

Mary Potter (dec.) w. of Christopher P. and Ambrose (50) and Marie (48) their children, by copy of 10 July 1625, parcels called Reeves Marsh and Reeves Meade, containing 6 ac., for lives. Rent 17s. Worth £5 3s.

Mary Potter (dec.) and Mary (48) her d., 10 ac. of meadow and pasture called Goosehill, for lives. Rent 17s. Worth £10 6s 8d.

Mary Potter, Ambrose P. and Mary P., as above, by copy of 27 Feb. 1609, a close called Grimsditch of 5 ac., for lives. Rent 4s 4d. Worth £3 15s 8d.

Mary Potter (48) and Ambrose P. (50), by copy of 3 Oct. 1612, ten. called Countishall and 2 closes called Loke containing 3½ ac., for lives. Rent, 2s. Worth £4 8s.

Mary Potter, Ambrose P. and Mary P., as above, by copy of 19 May 1608, certain land of the Barton containing 10 ac., for lives. Rent 5s 6d. Worth £5 4s 6d.

'TENEMENTS OF THE BARTON and for which there hath not beene produced any lease or coppie by the present occupiers.' Parke Place: Longe Meade, a meadow of 18 ac., 'the vesture or sheere' of 13 of which have been granted to various persons. The present tenant has vesture of 5 ac. and the 'after grass or lattermath' of the whole.

Middle Croft, 1 ac.; 2 little closes, 1 ac.; 2 parcels called the Little Lease Parkes, 4¾ ac.; Greate Lare Parke, 6¼ ac.; Greate waterleate, 5¼ ac.; Fatt Water Leate, 4⅛ ac.; Long Water Leate, 5 ac.; West Parke Marshe,

10 ac.; Middle Parke Marsh, 5 ac.; East Parke Marsh, 5 ac.; the Pease Arish, 4 ac.; the Barley Arish, 4½ ac.; Parke Close, 4½ ac.; Pound Close, 6¾ ac.; the Five Acres; Poole Close and the Bag Lease, both 12½ ac. All now held by William Morgan. In all 103⅛ ac. Rent £5 14s 8d. Worth £107 16s. Timber trees, saplings and pollards, in number 60, worth £9.

Parcel called the Marshe of 6½ ac.; 'vesture and sheere' of 2 ac. of meadow in Long Meade [Margl. note by William Webb: 'The premisses comprehended in this folio are granted by Coppy of Court Roll dureing the life of the said William Morgan, proved to be yet in being December 25 1650'.]; all occupied by Alexander Giles (75) who 'claimeth an estate for life and a reversionall estate for the life of Thomas Giles' (40). Rent 13s 4d, Worth £9 3s. [Margl. note[2]: 'by oath of Mr Eustace Budgell now worth onlely £7.']

North Close, 5⅛ ac.; Greate Close, 4¾ ac.; South Close, 1¾ ac.; Middle South Close, 3¾ ac.; Middle North Close, 5 ac.; Upper North Close, 3¼ ac.; Upper South Close, 2½ ac.; Lower Close, 2½ ac.; together 28½ ac. and ⅛. Occupied by Marmaduke Stubbs, in right of Mary (32) 'his now wife', for her life. [Endorsement by William Webb 'The coppy of the Reversion hath been produced and the said Mary proved to be alive'.]. Rent 15s. Worth £20 5s.

Samuel Sainthill gent. (22) claims 'vesture and sheere' of 1 ac. of meadow in Long Meade for life. [Marginal note: 'This clayme to be made good. This is affirmed by Eustace Budgell, Deputy Steward of the Mannor, upon his oath to be at this time letten for 12s per annum and beleveth it to be the true yearely value thereof.' 5 March 1660.] Rent 4s. Worth 18s.

Peter Wright (28), William W. (26) and John W. (28) claim 'vesture and sheere' of 1 ac. of meadow in Long Meade for lives. Rent 4s. Worth 18s.

Elizabeth Rowe (47) wid. claims 'vesture and sheere' of 1 ac. in Long Meade for life. Rent 4s. Worth 18s.

[Margl. note] A jury confirms that these were leaseholds; no copy produced; no certainty that copies were granted before 1641, 'which wee are informed some of them were not'.

FREEHOLDERS OF THE MANOR

Heirs of Sir Thomas Prideaux kt, in free soccage, lands called Rixmarsh, rent £1; Heirs of Sir William Kirkham, lands called Tirauncis in Bradninch parish, 4d; Edmond Reynell esq., mess. and land called Combe, 6d; Heirs of John Francis esq., 2 farthings of land, part of the Manor of Hele Paine [Hele Payne] in Bradninch parish, 6d; Peter Trosse esq., capital mess. called the Mansion House and land of Colebrooke [Colebrook], by affirmation consisting of 200 ac. in Collompton [Cullompton] parish, 6d; John Reymond esq., 2 mess. 2 curtelages and 50 ac. in Collompton parish, and a mess. and 100 ac. called Bagmoore [Bagmore] in Bradninch parish, 10s; Heirs of [—] Beare, part of a ten. called Goldhill, 2d; Francis Toogood, land called Bowhill [*id.*], 6d.

Total rents of assize   £1 12s 6d.

[2] Not in PRO copy.

COPYHOLDERS OF THE CUSTOMARY LANDS OF THE MANOR

Peter Pidsley (60) and Simon P. (dec.) s. of P. P., by copy of 29 Feb. 1620, ten. called Burnehaies of 67 ac. Rent 9s 8d. Worth £42 10s 4d. Trees, 60 in number, are worth £12.

Thomas Ware (66) and John Geere (dec.), by copy of 10 Aug. 1607, ten. in Combe of 26 ac., for lives. Rent 4s 2d. Worth £16 16s.
Reversion granted 11 Oct. 1633 to Henry W. (21) s. of T. W. for life.

Mary Shapcott (35) wid. of Henry S. gent., by virtue of her widow's estate, 2 ten. in Combe of 62½ ac. during widowhood. Rent 13s 10d. Worth £31 6s 2d.
Reversion granted 14 Oct. 1623 to Robert S. (30) and Margarett S. (32) s. and d. of H. S.

id., as above, ten. called Rode [*id.*] of 52 ac. Rent 6s. Worth £27 14s. Reversion granted as above.

Elizabeth Murch (40), wid. of Nicholas M., by virtue of widow's estate, ten. of Kentsmore of 56 ac. Rent 9s 8¼d. Worth £25.
Reversion granted 20 Aug. 1638 to William M. (20) s. of N. M. for life. Another reversion of the same date to Peter Murch (15), another s. of N. M. for life.

John Smith (58) and Thomas S. (dec.), by copy of 21 July 1612, moiety of ten. called Fordishaies [*id.*] of 22 ac., for lives. Rent 2s 6d. Worth £9 10s.

John Murch (40) and Nicholas M. (dec.), by copy of 10 Aug. 1622, ten. of Tedbridge [*id.*] of 86 ac. Rent 6s 9d. Worth £49 13s 3d.
Trees to the number of 80, worth £9.

id., by copy of 10 Aug. 1622, ten. of Lowdes of 44 ac., for lives. Rent 6s 9d. Worth £28. Eliza M. (40) w. of N. M. in possession by virtue of her widow's estate.

Nicholas Murch (dec.) and Clements M. (32), by copy of same date, ten. of Flesterhaies [*id.*] of 46 ac. for lives. Rent 9s 9d. Worth £30. Eliza M. has possession, as above. Timber trees worth £9.

Elizabeth Evans (66) wid. of John E., by virtue of her widow's estate, ten. called Hawdowne of 34 ac. Rent 4s 9d. Worth £16 15s 3d.

Reversion granted 14 Dec. 1631 to Ambrose Bone (dec.) s. of William B. and William (33) s. of Ambrose, for lives.

Sibill Murch (60) wid. of William M., by virtue of her widow's estate, ten. called Chapplehaies [Chapelhaies] of 71 ac. Rent 6s 10d. Worth £41 8s 4d. Reversion granted 11 April 1629 to John M. sn. (40) and John M. (20) his s. for lives. Trees numbering 80 are worth £16.

Richard Yeate (dec.) and John Y. (18), by copy of 30 Sept. 1634, the other moiety of ten. in Fordishaies, 'with the old mansion house with an oxehouse adjoyninge, on which side lyeth a curtelage late in the possession of Willmot Smith, with an old garden and orchard on the east and north parte late in the tenure of the foresaid Wilmot'; a close called Will Parke, 5 ac.; close called Waterleate, 2½ ac.; close called Little Downe, 3 ac.; parcel called the

Farthinge, 1 ac., for lives. Rent 2s 6d. Worth £8 10s. Grace Y. in possession by virtue of her widow's estate.

John Taylor (35) and Winifride Geere (40), by copy of 10 April 1634, ten. of Casebery [Caseberry] of 46 ac. for lives. Rent 6s 10d. Worth £32 12s 2d.

Sidwell Forst (50) wid. of [—] Forst, by virtue of her widow's estate, ten. in Casebery of 40 ac. Rent 8s 5d. Worth £16 12s.
Reversion granted 23 Aug. 1616 to John F. jn. (35) and Joane F. (dec.) for lives.

Robert Leigh and William L. (60) his s., by copy of 21 sept. 1592, 2 ten. called Quantishaies [*id.*] of 58 ac. for lives. Rent 17s 7d. Worth £36. William L. now in possession of part in virtue of a surrender by his f. Residue held by Katherine L. (50), wid. of Robert L., by virtue of her widow's estate.

Thomas Hill (80) and Henry H. (dec.), by copy of 25 Aug. [—] Eliz., 2 ten. called Oversekenhaies and Holmes totalling 54 ac., for lives. Rent 11s. Worth £35.
Reversion of the former ten. granted 16 Jan. 1630 to John H. sn. (42), s. of Thomas H., and John H. (dec.) s. of John H. for lives.
Reversion of the latter ten. granted, date as above, to Roger Hill (dec.) and George Hill (40) for lives.

Richard Warren (dec.) and Katherine W. (70) his sister and now the w. of John Salter, by copy of 17 May 1582, 2 ten. called Waterletowne of 94 ac. for lives. Rent 8s 8d. Worth £46 12s. Katherine W. is in possession.
Reversion granted 31 Dec. 1622 to Henry Salter (38) and Charles S. (36), sons of John and Katherine S. for lives.

John Weekes (36), by copy of 1 March 1615, ten. called Billings Moore [Billingsmoor] of 61 ac., for life. Rent 8s 2½d. Worth £36.
Reversion granted same date to Joan W. (44) and Honor W. (39).

John Weekes (36) and Honor W. (39) his s. [sic], by copy of 28 July 1604, ten. called Netherstenthaies alias Netherstowhaies of 31 ac. and 2 corn mills, for lives. Rent 8s. for the ten. and 10s for the mills. Worth £32.

Peter Warren (60) and Richard W. (27) his s., by copy of 31 Dec. 1636, ten. in Cranishaies of 35 ac., for lives. Rent 9s 9d. Worth £30.

The same, by copy of 4 April 1635, 2 ten. called Waterstane and Croselands of 84 ac. in all, for lives. Rent 15s 2d. Worth £63.
Trees, 758 in number, are worth £100.

Peter Warren (60) and Margaret (27) his d., by copy of 14 Dec. 1624, ten. called Horredge [Whorridge Farm] of 7 ac., for lives. Rent 1s 6d. Worth £5.

John Melhewish (40) and Richard M. (30) s. of John M., by copy of 31 Aug. 1625, ten. called Pacyscombe of 23 ac. for lives. Rent 4s 10d. Worth £14.

Joan Forse (60) and Mary F. d. of John F. (dec.), by copy of 15 Aug. 1588, 3 ten. called Wishay, Butland and Colforde of 115 ac. in all, for lives. Rent £1 1s 10d. Worth £59.
Reversion of a 'moiety by estimation of the three tenements (namely) the moyety of the entry of the house, the kitchen and the chamber on the same,

the milkhouse and the chamber on the same, the moiety of the curtelage, the barne and the little Shippen at the end of the barne, the stable and the swinehouse at the east end of the corte adjoyning to the greate orchard, the lynny in the Greene behinde the barne, the lynny adjoyinge to the east end of the barne thirty foote in length and thirty foote in breadth. Att the wester end of the house parte of the garden and close adjoyning the greene behinde the barne, the Little Crofte behinde the barne, the nursery adjoyninge to the Little Crofte, the moyety of the greate orchard, the Rudges, the North-downe, the Pitt Crofte, the Pitte Meade, the Home Meade, the Moore, the Little Close on the south of the Moore, the Well Parke, the Greate Long Crofte, the Five Acres, the Nether Waterleate, the Greate Stoke, the Cleavy Ball and the Round Ball', in all 61 ac. to Philip Moore jn. (28) and Willmott Moore (32), for lives. Rent, a moiety of the above rent, viz. 10s 11d. Reversion of the other moiety granted 14 Dec. 1631 to Alice Warren (28) and John W. (dec.), for lives. Rent, a moiety, as above.

John Forse (60), and John (25) and Holton (35) his s. and d., by copy of 20 Jan. 1624, 2 ten. called Gingerland [*id.*] of 91 ac. Rent 14s 10d. Worth £58.

Elizabeth Sumpter (60), and William (29) and Thomas (dec.) her s., by copy of 13 April 1637, ten. called Stoute [?Nether Stouthaies] of 46 ac., for lives. Rent 7s 2d. Worth £22.

Henry Shapcott (dec.) and Thomas Warren (70), by copy of 28 Sept. 1611, ten. called Downeheade [Downhead] of 62 ac. for lives. Rent 5s 3d. Worth £20. Trees numbering 150 worth £20.

Thomas Warren (70) and John W. (dec.), by copy of 12 Dec. 1577, 2 ten. called Chapplehaine [Chapelhaies] of 108 ac. for lives. Rent 13s 8d. Worth £74. Trees numbering 60 worth £9.

Philipe Moore sn. (28) and Mary M. (34), by copy of 5 Dec. 1631, ten. called Trinity [*id.*] of 26 ac. for lives. Rent 9s 2d. Worth £20.

Abigall Pearce (70) wid. of John P., by virtue of her widow's estate, ten. called Trinity of 28 ac. during her widowhood. Rent 6s 10d. Worth £16. Reversion granted 4 June 1612 to Thomas (dec.) and John (40) sons of J. P. for lives.

Clement Ridlake (dec.) and John R. (40) his s., by copy of 7 July 1604, 2 ten. called Cranishaies [*id.*] and Stonecombehaies, 66 ac. in all, for lives. Rent 12s. Worth £36. Trees numbering 140 worth £31.

Mary Moore (34) and Willmot M. (32) children of Phillip M., by copy of 17 July 1624, 2 ten. called Petterhaies and Sampsonhaies, together 30 ac., for lives. Rent 9s 6d. Worth £17.

John Baker (63) and Alice B. (30), by copy of 10 Aug. 1622, 2 ten. called Waterstawe [?Waterletown] of 27 ac., for lives. Rent 7s 6d. Worth £18. Trees numbering 100 worth £16.

Robert Wright (dec.) and William (40) his s., by copy of 16 Jan. 1612, ten called Weeke [*id.*] of 30 ac., for lives. Rent 3s 8d. Worth £14.

William Carpenter (59) and Agnes C. (dec.), by copy of 18 April 1594, ten.

called Northdowne [?Downs] of 19 ac. and a piece of land called Foxholes of 11 ac., for lives. Rent 12s. Worth £20.
Reversion of Northdowne granted 1 Oct. 1633 to John C. (22) s. of William, for life.
Reversion of Foxholes granted same date to said John C. and Mary (20) his s., for lives. Trees numbering 42 worth £6.

John Moore (70) and Phillip Moore (dec.) s. of Henry M., by copy of 10 Oct. 1588, 2 ten. called Hawkalter [Hawkealtar] and Loosebrooke, totalling 88 ac., for lives. Rent 8s 11d. Worth £40.
Reversion of Hawkealler granted 8 Oct. 1639 to Peter M. (28) for life.
Reversion of Losebrooke, same date, to William Wright (26) for life.

Francis Weeke (49) by copy of 12 March 1623, ten. called Stokehouse [*id.*] of 83 ac. for life. Rent 8s 1d. Worth £31.

Nicholas Burchill (40) by copy of 20 July 1628: ten. called Healthaies [Halthaies] of 31 ac. for life. Rent 9s 9d. Worth £32. Trees to the number of 106 worth £17.
Reversion granted 4 Feb. 1641 to Joan B. (39) w. of N. B. for life.

Hercules Gibb (72), by copy of 12 Nov. 1582, ten. called Bagmoore [Bagmore] of 33 ac. for life. Rent 6s 10d. Worth £17 15s 2d.
Reversion granted 28 March 1621 to Henry G. (45) and John G. (40) for lives.

Joan Colcherd (62) wid. of John C. by virtue of widow's estate, 2 ten. called Nelehaies [*id.*] and Cowslade in all 50 ac. Rent 6s 8d. Worth £34 16s.
Reversion granted 10 Oct. 1598 to Joan Colcherd (50) d. of John C. third s. of Thomasin C. and John C. (dec.) s. of John C. fourth s. of said Thomasin.

Petronel Warren (55) wid. of Richard W., by virtue of her widow's estate, ten. called Shevishaies [*id.*] of 38½ ac. Rent 7s 1½d. Worth £19 2s.
Reversion granted 25 Sept. 1623 to Joan Hill (50) and John H. (dec.).

Margerie Wright (38) d. of John W. and now w. of Calebb Saunders, by copy of 28 July 1613, ten. called Bowhill [*id.*] of 32 ac. for life. Rent 10s 11½d. Worth £19.
Calebb S. (40) claims an estate in the ten. for life by virtue of a copy of 14 April 1642. The 'jurors swear that Caleb contracted for estate for above tenn yeares before [20 Sept. 1649] and that the reason why the foresaid coppy was noe sooner graunted unto him was for that Peter Sainthill esq. the then Steward of the Mannor lay a long tyme sicke in the country.'

Edith Saunders (60) and Winifred Skinner (55), ds. of James Skinner by copy of 21 Oct. 1591, ten. called Sherehaies of 29 ac. for lives. Rent 7s 4d. Worth £18 3s 8d.

'CUSTOMARY TENEMENTS OF THE SAID MANNOR FOR WHICH THERE HATH NOE COPPIES BEENE PRODUCED BY THE PRESENT OCCUPIERS'
Ten. of 32 ac. called Battins [Bathaics] in possession of Thomas Harecourte (18) and John (14) his br. who claim the estate. Rent 9s 9d. Worth £28 10s 3d. Trees numbering 80 worth £13 11s. 8d.

Ten. called Bythawin occupied by Henry Harcourte (13) of 32 ac. Henry H.

and Thomas [see above] his br. claim an estate for lives. Rent £1. Worth £20 11s 6d. Trees numbering 140 worth £12.

Ten. called Champerhaies of 60 ac. occupied by John Crosse (23), who claims an estate for life. Rent 14s 4d. Worth £59 5s 8d. Trees numbering 140 worth £22 13s 4d.

Md. 'The jury swear the aforesaid to be tenants by copy for life, but have produced no copy and we are informed that the said copies were granted in 1641 or since.'

'BURROUGHE OF BRADNINCHE

'The said Burroughe lieth within the boundes of the said Mannor of Bradninche . . . and is governed by a Mayor and Burgesses whoe hold theire priveledges by charter which was renewed unto them in the reigne of the late King James, out of which Burroughe there is collected and paid by the Mayor for all the burgages thereof as a quitt rent p.a.' £7 4s 7d.
'There is also paid by the Burgesses . . . upon any death or alienacon for a relieffe double the rent of such burgage of which the present tenant died seized or alienated, the which relieffes with the perquisites of courte which alsoe belongeth to the Lord will amount' on av. to £1 4s.

Total of rents and perquisites   £8 8s 7d.

'COMONS BELONGING TO THE SAID MANNOR

'There is a certeine parcell of land called Bradninch Comon conteyninge [20 ac.] in which all the customarie tennants viz. the coppie-holders of the Mannor claime to have right of Comon for the depastureing of horses, sheepe and all other cattle at theire pleasure and alsoe to have free liberty to take estovers without number for theire severall uses.

BOUNDES OF THE SAID MANNOR

The said Mannor is bounded on the east side with the Mannor of Sir John Poke barronett called Aller Peverell [in Kentisbeare] on the south side, with the Mannor of Hele Paine [Hele Payne] being the lands of the heires of John Fraunces esq. dec., on the west side with the lands of Sir John Strangewaies kt, William Windham esq., Henry Skibbowe and John Land gent. and on the north side with the lands of Symon Heathe esq.'

CUSTOMS

A Court Leet is held twice a year and a Court Baron every three weeks, to which all free and customary tenants owe suit and service.
Freeholders owe a relief, which is double their rent, on every death or alienation. A customary tenant owes a best beast as a heriot for each tenement that he holds, 'which said harriott is to be apprized by foure of the customarie tennants, and the tenant in reversion is to have it at anothers price giveing securitie by two tennants for the value of it. But on such tennants refusall the Lord may take his best Chapman for the same, which said relieffes and herriotts with the fines, issues . . . will amount [on av.] to £10.'
Customary tenants hold by copy of the Court Roll 'for one life in possession and two lifes in reversion and . . . if there be two tennants of one tenement,

the one in possession and the other in reversion, if the tennant in possession doe surrender (which the Steward is not to refuse) all his tenement into the hands of the Lord of the Mannor for tyme being unto him in reversion upon condicon that they both may be admitted joynt tennants of the whole with a provisoe that the reversioner shall manure onely such parte of the tenement as the tennant first in possession shall nominate in Courte dureing the life of the said first tennant in possession, and the widowes estate of such woman as shalbe his wiefe at the day of his death. And after such surrender made the Lord . . . may graunt the reversion for one or two lives of such tenement soe surrendered. But if there be any estate graunted of any tenement unto two persons by one coppie for terme of theire lives successively then by the custome of this Mannor the Lord cannott graunt anie reversion of such estate untill they both be admitted as tennants or one of them die.'

A widow may continue to occupy her late husband's tenement during her widowhood, 'but if she marry againe then the said tenement . . . is to fall to the next life in reversion if there be anie.'

If a customary tenant surrenders the whole or part of his tenement to the tenant in reversion, the Lord is to receive from the tenant surrendering 3s 4d for his leave, and the Steward 2d for entering the surrender, and the Reeve 4d for his attendance.

If a customary tenant 'hath a minde to sett or lett any parte or his whole tenement he must first desire leave at the Courte from the Lord or Steward or his deputie, and upon payment of six pence to the Lord and one penny to the Steward he is to have a coppy of lycence to sett all or any parte of his tenement dureing the life of such tennant.'

If a tenant needs timber for necessary repairs to his tenement, the Reeve is to deliver the same. 'And when an estate is grauntable by the Lord the tennant in possession is first to refuse the takeing thereof before the Lord cann graunt the same to any other in revercion.'

OFFICERS

There hath beene accustomed to be a High Steward of the said Mannor whoe hath by himselfe graunted estates by coppie of Corte Rolle, which said Steward is put in by the Lord . . . and is to continue soe long as the said Lord shall please.'

'Under him there is accustomed to be an Under Steward or Courte Keeper whoe hath beene formerly allowed five poundes for his fee, but this is at the Lords pleasure.'

'Alsoe there is a Reeve chosen every yeare out of the customary tenants whoe is to execute the said office upon oathe, and is alsoe to collect the Lords rents [and prequisites, etc.] for which he hath beene alwaies allowed' 3s 2$\frac{1}{4}$d.

An Abstract of the present Rents, future Improvements and other Profits arising out of the said Honour, Manor and Borough

Respite of homage, paid by free tenants who hold of the Honour	£1	10s	
Rents of assize and perquisites	£11	7s	6d
Rents of copyholders who have produced their copies	£19	0s	0$\frac{3}{4}$d
Rents of copyholders without copy	£2	4s	1$\frac{3}{4}$d

Rents of copyholders of the Barton	£19	14s	8d
Rents of Barton copyholders without copy	£7	14s	11d
Rents and perquisites of the borough	£8	8s	7d
Rents of leasehold tenements	£1	15s	
Total	£71	14s	10½d
Improved value of the reliefs of the Honour	£6	13s	4d
Improved value of Barton copyhold tenements	£925	10s	4d
Improved value of Barton copyholds without copy	£121	18s	
Improved value of Manor copyhold tenements	£762	6s	4d
Improved value of manorial copyholds without copy	£101	7s	4d
Improved value of leasehold tenements	£60		
Total improved value	£1845	17s	4d[3]
Timber trees, etc. worth	£342	5s	

56 THE PORT AND WATER LIBERTIES OF DARTMOUTH, DEVON

DCO S/8; PRO E 317 (D)/7. Jurisdiction over the navigable River Dart was vested in the Duchy from its inception.

'A Survey of the Port, Water, Liberties and precincts of the Towne or Borroughe of Dartmouth alias Clifton Dartmouth Hardness in the Countie of Devon parcell of the Dukedom of Cornewall . . . retorned [7 Oct. 1650].

All that the office of Water Bayliffe of the Towne of Borroughe of Dartmouth . . . with all and singular the petty customes belonginge to the said office, viz. for every tonne of all manner of wynes comeing within the Port or Water of Dartmouth sixe pence; for every tonne of iron eight pence; for every tonne of fruite eight pence; for every peece of Cressey cloth two pence; for every hundred of canvas two pence; for every barrell of blacke sope one penny; for every barrell of herrings one half penny; for every barrell of pitche one halfe penny; for every barrell of tarr one halfe penny; for every bale of mader foure pence; for every bale of woade two pence; for every pipe of woade eight pence; for every hundred of broade fish two pence; for every hundred of hakes or rayes one penny; for every packe of woolen clothe foure pence; for every peece of broadcloth one penny halfe penny; for every cloth in Kerseys one penny halfe penny; for every hundred of white tinn two pence; for every quarter of salt, wheate, malt, coles and all manner of grayne and all other merchandise valued to be worth twentie shillings two pence; for every shipp that is bought or sould into or out of the land sixe shillings eight pence; for every balinger bought or sould into or out of the land three shillings foure pence. And all and all manner of rights, authorities profitts, comodities, revenues and emoluments to the said office belonging or in any wise apperteyninge.

All which the foresaid premisses and office of Water Bayliffe aforesaid are graunted by Letters Pattents beareing date at Westminster [4 March 1626] unto the Major, Bayliffes and Burgesses of the foresaid Towne or Borrough

---
[3] The arithmetic is incorrect.

of Dartmouth and to theire successors with power and authoritie for the chooseing, makeing [. . .] of the said Towne to the office of Under Water Bayliffe when, as often and as long as they shall please. Habend', gaudend' et exercend' the said office and premisses for the terme of ninety nine yeares if John Plumbleigh (32) sonne of William Plumbleigh sen., John Mathew (33) sonne of Roger Mathew, and Robert Jagoe (43) sonne of Pascatius Jayne or one of them should soe long live.' Rendering at the accustomed times £14 13s 4d. The improved value besides the present rent p.a. £6 6s 8d.

'It is provided that if the said rent shalbe unpaid by the spane of fortie daies after it shall grow due that then this graunt shalbe voide.'

'This is an exact survey . . . [sd].

57   BOROUGH OF LYDFORD, DEVON

DCO S/8; PRO E 317 (D)/9. The borough and manor of Lydford were vested in the Duchy from its inception, together with the Forest of Dartmoor which was not surveyed at this time. They were counted amongst the *forinseca maneria*.

'A Survey of the Borrough of Lidford . . . within the County of Devon, parte of the Dutchie there . . . retorned [27 Aug. 1650].

Lidford Castle

The said castle is very much in decay and almost totally ruined. The walls are built of lime and stone, within the compasse of which walls there is foure little roomes where of to are above staires, the flore of which is all broken, divers of the cheifest beames being fallen to the ground and all the rest is following, only the roofe of the saide Castle (being lately repaired by the Prince and covered with lead) is more substantiall than the other parts.

The scite of the said Castle with the ditches and courte conteyne halfe an acre of land of which the Burrough of Lidford holdeth the courte at the will of the Lord, for which they pay the yearly rent of twelve pence. The said scite is valued to be worth at an improvement besides the foresaid rent p.a. 5s.

The stones about the said Castle are not worth the takeing downe, but there are divers parcells of old timber which we value to be worth de claro £6.
There is one parte of the tower leaded conteyning [1445] square feete; every foote conteyneth (by weight) nine pounds; in all [13,895] poundes which at a penny halfpenny a pound cometh to [£86 16s 10½d]. But consideration being had to the taking of it downe and the portage we reprise [£6 16s 10½d], so then it amounteth to de claro [£80].

Lidford Burrough

The quite rent or rents of assize of the said Burroughe doe amonte to yearly the sume of [£3 1s 4d] parte of which said rents (vizt three pounds) is paide to the Rector of the parish of Lidford in leue of all the tythes of the Forrest of

Dartmoore, soo that the cleare rent accruing to the Lord amounteth to the yearly rent of [1s 4d].

The said Burrough doth pay to the Lord for the faire that is yearly held there, vizt at the feast of St Bartholomew, the sume of [1s 6d].

There is alsoe paide by the said Burrough for alewaights the sume of [1s] p.a.

So that the whole rent which the said Burrough payeth to the Lord with the one shilling for the Castle Greene amounteth to p.a. [£4 10s].

There is belonginge to the said Burrough a Watter Mill knowne by the name of Lidford Mill which was granted to Sir Thomas Reynell kt by [L. P. of 9 June 1626 for 31 years at a rent of £1 10s]. The said Mill is now very much out of repaire and almost totaly ruined by reason of the late warres, but we are informed that the said mill before the troubles (vizt in the yeare 1640) was let out for [£20] yearly (it being then in good repaire) soe that the improvement of the said mill (after the foresaid rate) besides the rent amounteth to p.a. [blank].

There is to be reprised to the purchaser to erecte the said mill (it being now totaly ruined) the sume of [£55].

The said Sir Thomas Reynell kt . . . did assigne . . . the foresaid mill with the appurtenances unto Sir James Baggs kt, who did assigne it unto Sir Nicholas Slanning kt, who being one disaffected to the state and in actuall armes for the late King, it was sequestred by the Comittee for the County of Devon (and so now it standeth) and was by the said Comittie let out to farme to Mr John Champ[. . .]y, afterwards to Mr James Pearce who now hath it and payeth the rent reserved for it.

There is lying within the said Burrough certaine land heretofore John Denhams esq., who dying without issue male, lefte it to be devided be-tweene two daughters one of which dyed (not being married) without heire leaving behinde her a basse sonne, soe that her moyety of land was esche-ated to the respective Lords in whose mannors it laye (a basterd not being to inherite). The land that lyeth within this Burrough conteyneth seven acres, the moyety of which (viz 3½ ac.) is escheated to the Lord thereof which is valued to be worth three pounds yearly.

The said land was lett in lease by the foresaid Denham (before the time of his death) unto William Pellow of the towne of Lidford as appeareth by an indenture [dated 30 Nov. 1639, for the term of 99 years, on the lives of James Gill (45), s. of John Gill of the parish of Bridstow [Bridestowe] and Katherin (dec.) his w., at a rent of 10s for the whole] out of which five shillings is payable to the state for the moyety escheated so that the improvement of the said land cometh to beside the present rent' p.a. £2 15s 0d.

'CUSTOMES OF THE SAID BURROUGH

There is kept severall courtes yearely . . . to which all that hold any land within the Burrough are bounde to doe suite and service.'

Perquisites of court, reliefs and other casualties amount p.a. to 5s, '. . . the heire of every tennement at his taking the possession of his prediccessors lands paying fifteene pence in leue of a relleife.'

ABSTRACT OF THE PRESENT RENT AND FUTURE
IMPROVEMENTS OF THE BOROUGH

Quit rent, other rents and perquisites of court	£2 4s 10d
Improvement of the Castle Ditches and Castle Greene	5s
Improvement of the mills of the borough	£20
Improvement of escheated lands now in lease, p.a.	£2 15s
Value of future improvements of the Borough	£23
Timber in the Castle	£6
Lead in the Castle	£80

'This is an exact survey . . . [sd].

Stitched to this survey is one dated Nov. 1658. It is summarised here:

Quite rents	£9 13s 4½d
Perquisites of court, heriots, reliefs, etc.	£1 10s 0d

'There is due upon every alienacion in fee one yeares quitt rent for a reliefe unto the Lord over and above the due rent and upon death of every tenante a like reliefe.
The premisses are the discovery of Robert Fisher gent.'[1]

58 THE HONOURS OF OKEHAMPTON AND PLYMPTON, DEVON

DCO S/8; PRO E 317 (D)/10. The Honours of Okehampton and Plympton escheated to the Crown on the attainder of Henry Courtenay, Marquis of Exeter, in 1538, and were attached to the Duchy in 1540. Apart from the fee of Week St Mary in North Cornwall, the Honours consisted only of the military obligations of their free tenants.

'A Survey of the Honors of Okehampton and Plimpton with the Fee of Weeke St Mary lying . . . in the Counties of Devon and Cornewall, parte of the possessions of Charles Stuart the late King but now settled on Trustees . . . retorned [27 Nov. 1650].

All that the Honor of Okehampton of which there is held [90] knights fees, three partes whereof in eight equally devided belonged to the late King unto whom there hath beene formerly paid by the free tennants whoe hold of the said Honnor for garrett money and suite of corte yearely as a quitt rent' p.a. £12 10s 10d.

'The relieffes ariseing and groweing due within this Honnor . . . did amount unto [on av. £11 5s] out of which there being deducted three partes in eight as aforesaid there remained to be paid to the late King' p.a. £6 17s 6d.

'All that the Honnor of Plimpton lying in the County of Devon of which there is held [120] knights fees, three partes whereof in eight partes equally devided belonged to the late King unto whom there hath beene heretofore paid for garrett money and suite to Corte by the free tennants whoe hold of the said Honnor yearely as a quitt rent' p.a. £14 2s.

[1] The fact that these rents also belonged to the Duchy was made known to the Trustees by Robert Fisher.

'The relieffes ariseing and groweing due within the Honnor of Plimpton did amount unto [on av. £15] out of which there being deducted five partes in eight, there remained to be paid to the late King' p.a. £5 12s 6d.

'All that the fee of Weeke St Mary [*id.*] lying . . . in the Counties of Cornewall and Devon, the whole whereof belonged to the late King whoe purchased the same of Christopher Pollard esq., but now many knights fees are held of the said fee wee cannott come to the knowledge of, neither what rent or respitt of homage hath beene yearely answered wee cannott find out, there haveing beene nothing paid by the tennants of the said fee since the same was purchased of the said Pollard.'

Reliefs within the fee of Week St Mary are p.a. on av. £1 10s.

William Skinner holds a ten. or burgage in 'the Burroughe of Weeke St Mary' by lease from Christopher Pollard esq. dated 1 June 1610 for 99 years on lives of Joan (79), w. of W. S., and John (50) and Temperance (dec.) their children. Rent 3s 4d. Heriot 13s 4d. Impr. val. £1.

Joan Wills wid. claims an estate in another ten. by grant from C. Pollard, 'which was not produced unto us'. It is worth p.a. 6s 8d.

'All which the foresaid Honnor and fee (with all appurtenances)' are granted to Ninian Cunningham gent. by L. P. dated 6 June 1635, for a term of 31 years. Rent £6 13s 4d. Impr. val. 'if the said rents be continued and relieffes paid', £35 6s 2d.
Excepted from the grant 'all wardes, fines for wardes [and] marriages, and graunts of the lands of wards happening in any of the aforesaid fees or either of them.'
The grant is void if the rent remains unpaid for 40 days.

The fee of Week St Mary was assigned by Mr Cuningham to Richard Langford, 20 Feb. 1639 for the remainder of the term at a rent of 'one shilling if lawfully demanded'.

'A perfect returne of the said honnors and fee.'

[Endorsed] All above assigned by Cunningham 7 July 1648 to Thomas Strechleigh of London for the remainder of the term.

59   MANOR OF SHEBBEAR, DEVON

PRO E 317 (D)/11. The small manor of Shebbear, lying in the parish of that name in north west Devon, had been part of the Neville estates, and escheated to the Crown under Henry VII.[1]

'A Survey of the Mannor of Shebbeare alias Shaftisbury . . . retorned [10 Sept. 1650].

All that capitall messuage knowen by the name of Bradworthy [Badworthy] with the moiety of lands thereunto belonginge, conteyninge [180 ac.] of

[1] See part 1, p. xvi.

meadow, arable, pasture and moorish ground, with the profitts etc. . . . now or late in the tenure and occupation of Thomas Hutchins, and is valued to be worth' p.a. £32.

The other moiety, of 117 ac., and a mill known as Bradworthy Mill, occupied by Robert Hutchins, worth £24.

Land or agistment called Vale Vade of 25 ac., occupied by Robert Hutchins, worth £9.

Moorish ground called Bradworthy Moor, of 180 ac., occupied by Anne Davill, worth £5.

Ten. called Berry of 40 ac., occupied by Joseph Grigg and Christopher Holmoore, worth £15.

Ten. called Penknowle [Pennickhold] of 37 ac., occupied by Jane Allen wid. worth £15 14s.

Ten. called Loverscott [Lovacott], of 24 ac., occupied by 'Yeo', worth £6.

Ten. called South Combe of 95 ac., occupied by Robert Markham worth £20.

Ten. called Vada Cutt Corner [Vaddicott] of 4½ ac., occupied by George Ascutt, worth £3.

Ten. called Coate of 14 ac., occupied by Ciprian Whitefield, worth £6.

Ten. in Coate [Caute] of 21 ac., occupied by John Saunders, worth £5.

Ten. called Wotton [Wootton] of 145 ac., occupied by Thomas Badcocke, worth £21 13s.

'All which the foresaide premisses were let by the late King to Sir John Gill kt and Thomas Brewer gent., by L. P. of 7 July 1630 for 100 years. Rent £5. Impr. val. besides the present rent £157 11s 6d.

Md. 'that Thomas Gifford, sonne and heire of Thomas Gifford of Halisbury deceased claimes the foresaid lands as his owne proper right and as a parte of his inheritance, which he saith he will make appear by sufficient evidences.'

'This is an exact survey . . . [sd].

Added by William Webb: 'The premisses comprehended in this survey are prooved to be the inheritance of the said thomas Gifford, and that the Crowne had never anye proffitt thereof.' Oct. 28 1650.

60   MILLS IN SIDMOUTH, DEVON

PRO E 317 (D)/13. It is not known how these three mills in Sidmouth in south-eastern Devon passed into the possession of the Crown.

'A retorne of three mills called Sydmouth Mills lying . . . in the Mannor of Sydmouth . . . parcell of the possessions of the late King . . . retorned [25 Nov. 1650].

William Lee holdeth by coppie of corte rolle [of 25 July 1628] all those three water corne mills . . . in the Mannor of Sydmouth with theire apputenances and the suite of mulcture of the tennants of the said Mannor' for life, aged 71. Rent £4 13s 4d. Worth besides the present rent p.a. £45 6s 8d.

'The reversion of the said mill is claimed to be graunted by coppy not produced onto Edmond Prideaux esq., for the terme of his life by the rent and services aforesaid.'

'This is a perfect retorne of the said mills' [Sd. Crompton did not sign this survey]

Md. 'This claime to be made good by order of the Committee of Parliament for Removing Obstructions entered on the backside of this sheete. This claime is allowed.'

Endorsement, dated 4 Feb. 1650: 'At the Committee of Parliament for removing Obstructions in the Sale of Honours . . . of the late King, Queene and Prince.

Forasmuch as this Committee have this day read and taken into consideracon the petition of Edmond Prideaux esq., Attourney Generall for the Commonwealth and also a copie of court rolle made at a Court baron held within the Mannor of Sydmouth . . . [9 Aug. 1627], by which copie it appeares unto this Committee that the said Mr Attourney Generall by the name of Edmond Prideaux the younger is admitted to an estate in revertion in certaine corne mills called Sydmouth Mills with thappurtenances within the said Mannor, to hold the same to him and his eldest sonne for their lives successively by the rent and services accustomed after the death, surrender or forfeiture or other determination of William Lee, Thomas and Zachary Lee, sonnes of the said William Lee. It is the opinion of this Committee, and so ordered that the said copie and the interest granted thereby in and to the said mills . . . be allowed of; and the Surveyor Generall for sale of the said honours . . . doe enter and record upon the survey of the said Mannor the said interest, and that the said lives are now in being.'

Entered 10 Feb. 1650. Sd. William Monson
      William Say
      H. Edwards
      John Bourchier
      James Chaloner

61   MANOR OF SOUTH TEIGN

DCO S/8; PRO E 317 (D)/12. The manor of South Teign lay in Chagford parish. The place-name has been lost, but the manor is probably to be identified with Teigncombe.[1] It was acquired by the Duchy in 1342, and counted as one of the *forinseca maneria*.

'A Survey of the Mannor of Southteigne . . . retorned [26 Nov. 1650].

Demeasnes belonging to the said Mannor

All that water grist mill lying . . . in Weake [Great Week] with a garden thereto adjoyninge in the possession of Elizabeth Glanvile wid. and Francis her son, who claime an estate therein for certeine yeares yet to come, but produced noe lease or other graunt for the same. Which said mill being fallen into decay and quite out of repaire the same is worth noe more than the present rent' of 10s.

'All that parcell of woodground called Horselake [*id.*] Woode, the pasture whereof the tennants of Horselake Wood claimed to be theires by the rent of one shilling. Which said wood conteyneth tenn acres and the wood that formerly grewed thereon being wholely destroied, there remaines noe more thereof to the Lord but the soile, but if the tennants cannott make good theire claime to the pasturage thereof wee value it to be worth' p.a. £1 10s.

'Free-tennants of the said Mannor

Sir John Whiddon kt holdeth in free soccage to him and his heires for ever divers messuages, lands and tenements within the parishes of Morton [Moretonhampstead], Northbovie [North Bovey] and Chagford [*id.*], conteyning by estimacion [800 ac.] for which he paieth' p.a. £2 16s 2d.

id., 3 parts of a ten. to be divided into seven parts, containing altogether 37 ac. in Westcott [*id.*]; Oliver Cliffe hold 3 parts, and John Geales and [—] his w. hold the seventh part. Rent 3s 3½d.

Oliver Whiddon esq., a ten. called Whiddon of 40 ac. 'or thereabout', 3s 5½d.

id., part of a ten. called Ford; the heirs of William Newcombe the rest, 6s 8d.

Thomas Collihole, 3 parts of a ten. of 63 ac. called Hearne, in Easton [*id.*], divided into 9 parts; Stephen Bennett a ninth; Oliver Whiddon the other 5 parts, except a cott. and a meadow called Broade Meade which Elizabeth Knapman and Margarett Newcombe, daughters and heirs of William Newcombe hold, 7s.

Oliver Whiddon, 1 part of a ten. in Easton, 18 ac.; the heirs of William Newcombe the rest, 6s 6d; *id.*, ten. called Thorne in Northbovie [North Bovey] parish of 53 ac., 5s 2½d; Thomas Bennett, ten. in Easton called Shutte of 30 ac., 3s 3½d; John Noseworthy, ten. in Easton of 40 ac., 3s 2½d; Nicholas Laskey, a close called Whittaberry [Whiteabury] of 18 ac., 2s 4d; Phillipp Smith,[2] ten. in Westcott of 35 ac., 3s 3½d; Thomas Bennett, ten. part of which lies in Little Weeke and part in Broad Weeke, of 30 ac., 2s 6d; John Will, another ten. in Little and Broad Week [Great

[1] See Part 1, p. xv.
[2] DCO—'Symth'.

Week], of 30 ac., 2s 6d;   Thomas Veldon, ten. in Broad Weeke, of 53 ac.,
5s 2½d;   *id.*, ten. in Middlecott of 53 ac., 4s 8½d;   *id.*, moiety of ten. in
Woode [Woodtown] of 20 ac., 1s 6d;   Thomas Denford, moiety of ten. in
Wood of 20 ac., 1s 6d;   John Hooper, ten. in Broade Weeke of 53 ac.,
5s 2½d;   Edward Ellis, ten. in Ellam of 34 ac., 3s 4¼d;   Edward Furlonge
and Robert Chaffe gent. in right of their wives, ten. in Meacombe [*id.*] in
Morton   Hampsteade   [Moretonhampstead]   parish,   of   40   ac.,
5s 11d;   Thomas Croute, ten. in Horselake, of 20 ac., 2s 0¼d;   Robert
Foxford, ten. in Thorne [Thorn], of 53 ac., 5s 2½d;   John Fowell, ten. 'or
certeine closes of land called Clerkes Parkes' of 9 ac., 2d;   John Vallance,
ten. in Middlecott, of 53 ac., 4s 8½d;   John Endacott, ten. in Throwson of
65 ac., 7s 4d;   *id.*, ten. in Middlecott, of 53 ac., 4s 8½d;   Thomas Taver-
nor, ten. in Throwson of 70 ac., 7s 4d;   *id.*, a meadow in Greenewill of 2 ac.,
2d;   John Ellis, a ten. in Greenewill of 50 ac., 3s 2½d;   *id.*, a close called
Combe Parke and a ten in Middlecott of 22 ac., 2s 4¼d;   *id.*, piece of land
called Ellacombe Downe, of 12 ac., 2s 2d;   John Lyne, ten. in Middlecott
of 27 ac., 2s 4¼d;   John Cornish, 3 ten. in Slancombe of about 90 ac.,
9s 8½d;   *id.*, moiety of another ten. in Slancombe of about 15 ac.,
1s 7¼d;   John Steene, a ten. and a moiety of another in Slancombe of
45 ac., 4s 9½d;   Thomas Hill, ten. and half a ten. in Slancombe of 45 ac.,
4s 9¼d;   William Hill, moiety of ten. in Slancombe of 15 ac.,
1s 7¼d;   Richard Cornish, ten. in Slancombe of 30 ac., 3s 3½d;   Richard
Wannell, piece of land in Slancombe of 2 ac., 2d.

'There is paid out of a certeine tenement called Lakeland [*id.*] unto the Lord
of this Mannor as a high rent', 2s 6d;   From ten. at Buckland as a quit rent,
1s;   'for a certeine ware called Shilston Ware [Weir] as a quit rent',
1s;   'And alsoe for Scobbletorre by the occupiers thereof', 1s;   'by the
tennants of Horselake and Wood [sic] for pasturage of Horslakewood', 1s.

                                        Total   £10 5s.

'BOUNDES OF THE SAID MANNOR OF SOUTHTEIGNE
The said Mannor is bounded on the east side with the Mannor of Palford
[Pafford], on the south east by the Mannor of Morton [Moretonhampstead]
and on the south by parcell of the Mannor of Ippelpen [Ipplepen] within
the parish of North Bovie [North Bovey], on the south west with the
Mannor of Shapley Hellion and the Mannor of Shapley [*id.*], on the west
with the Mannor of Chagford [*id.*], and on the north with the Mannor of
Rushford [*id.*] and Shilston [?Shilstone in Throwleigh] lyinge by the River
of Teigne.'

CUSTOMS OF THE MANOR
Court Leet, View of Frankpledge and a three-weekly Court Baron have
been kept, to which all 'free tennants which hold a capitall messuage upon
lawful summons are bound to doe theire suite'.
A relief consisting of one year's rent on every alienation and on the death of
each free tenant. Reliefs, with heriots and other perquisites amount on av.
to £1 12s, 'besides five shillings paid to the Bayliffe for the collecting
thereof'.
When a free tenant dies his lands and tenements pass to his heir, but his

widow 'hath her dower by agreement with the heire and in default thereof by writt in the Courte of the same Mannor'.

A bailiff is chosen each year to collect rents, reliefs, heriots, etc., and 'is to be allowed by the Lord five shillings'.

AN ABSTRACT OF THE PRESENT RENTS AND IMPROVEMENTS
OF THE MANOR

Rents of assize and perquisites	£11 17s
Value of the mill	10s
Value of Horselake in addition to the rent paid for pasturage	£1 10s
Total	£13 17s

'This is an exact survey . . . [Sd].'

62   WATER AND POOL OF SUTTON, PLYMOUTH, DEVON

DCO S/7; PRO E 317 (D)/16. Jurisdiction over the harbour of Sutton (Plymouth) was part of the original privileges of the Duchy.

'A Survey of the Water and Poole of Sutton . . . parte of the auntient Dukedome of Cornewall . . . retorned [7 Oct. 1650].

All that the Water and Poole of Sutton with the profitts of the same (vizt) anchorage and keeleage of every shipp entering within the Poole aforesaid or toucheing the land there; messurage or bushelage of every shipp entring within the Poole aforesaid fraighted with any kind of corne or grayne, malt or salt or any such thing and valued there; lastage of every shipp unladed within the Poole aforesaid; the fine of twelve pence yearely of every fisher boate takeing fish and coming in the Water and Poole aforesaid; and pottage, (vizt) all those fines of fish juters for which it was agreed by the said juters and also all somes of money and other fees, duties and profitts for the said anchorage, keelage, measurage, bushelage, lastage, fines of fisher boates and pottage due and payable or appurteyninge to the said Poole and Water of Sutton.'

Granted by L. P. of 14 June 1628 to Sir John Walter, Sir James Fullerton and Sir Thomas Trevor, for 20½ years [corrected from 31] from 25 March 1638. Rent £13 6s 8d to the Duchy. Worth besides the present rent £6 13s 4d.

Lease assigned 17 March 1629 to Thomas Caldwell esq., who assigned it 20 Dec. 1634 to Sir David Cunningham, who assigned it 27 March (. . .) to Peter Hendra of Plympton St Mary gent., who assigned it 25 July 1640 'to the Governor, Assistants, Wardens and poore people of the Hospital of Orphans Aide in the Borroughe of Plymmouth, who are in possession.'

Md. 'that there are divers houses built upon the brinckes of the said Poole and within the highwater marke thereof, but whether they are built within the precincts of the same Poole wee cannot receave any certeine informacion, the Mayor and Burgesses of the Borroughe aforesaid claimeing all the land adioyning to the said Poole and being above the low water marke to be a parte of the Mannor of Sutton Prior of which they are Lords.

This is an exact survey . . . [Sd].

63   MANOR OF WEST ASHFORD, DEVON

PRO E 317 (D)/14. The manor lay in the parish of Heanton Punchardon. It passed to the Crown in 1554 following the attainder of Henry Gray, Duke of Suffolk.

'A Survey of the Mannor of West Ashford . . . parte of the possessions of Charles Stuarte the late King, but now setled on trustees . . . retorned [5 Nov. 1650].

There have bine heretofore divers free tennants within the said Mannor, but in regarde there hath not bine any corte for a long time helde within the same the names of the free tennants, what they are, what land they hold and what rents they pay are quite lost, but the coppieholders of the said Mannor are as follow:'

Thomas Cocke gent., by copy, ten. and a moiety of another in Cholwell of 22 ac., for lives of himself (41), and of Thomas (15) his s. and Mary (17) his d. successively. Worth £14.

James Dallyn (60), by copy, ten. in West Ashford of 15 ac., for lives of himself and Alexander (23) his s. Worth £8.

Alexander Dallyn (23), by copy, another ten. in West Ashford of 15 ac., for lives of himself and Ellynonor (24) his sister successively. Worth £8.

John Valicote, by copy, ten. in West Ashford of 28 ac. for lives of William Valicot (30), Jeoffery V. (23) and John V. (26) successively. Worth £15.

John Fairechilde, by copy, a ten. and a moiety of another in West Ashford of 28 ac. for lives of William F. (33), Robert F. (14) and John F. (18). Worth £15.

John Pillarin (40), by copy, 2 ten. in West Ashford of 28 ac. for lives of himself, Amos Partridge (26) and Ambrose Red (30). Worth £15.

Mary Norris (56), by copy, ten. in West Ashford of 14 ac. for lives of herself, William (24) and John (30) [her sons?] successively. Worth £8.

Margaret Sanders (45), by copy, ten. in West Ashford of 14 ac. for lives of herself and Phillip (11) and John (10) [her sons?]. Worth £8.

Thomas French (36), by copy, ten. and moiety of another in West Ashford of 28 ac. for lives of himself and Henry F. (4) and Mary F. (2) [his children?]. Worth £15.

Joan Bilsworthy (60), by widow's estate, ten. in West Ashford of 14 ac. Worth £8.

Ralph Wilkey (50), by copy, ten. in West Ashford of 14 ac. by lives of himself and Margaret Hayward (48). Worth £8.

All these premises were granted by L. P. of 24 Feb. 1627 to Sir Thomas Gorges for 41 years to begin after the death of Helene Marchioness of Northampton. Rent £11 18s 3d. Worth besides the present rent £120. Gorges has power to grant by copy any of the foresaid tenements when and to whom he pleases.

Exceptions, etc.

Md. The Marchioness of Northampton died 1 April 1635.

Sir Thomas Gorges assigned the lease to John Cholomore by indenture of 20 Nov. 1639. J. C. is the present tenant and is in possession.

'This is an exact survey . . . [Sd, but not by Crompton]

64   WEST ASHFORD, DEVON

PRO E 317 (D)/15.

'An additionall survey of the Mannor of West Ashford. . . retorned [29 Jan. 1651].

There are within the aforesaid Mannor divers cottages which the coppyhold tennants by licence of the lord have built upon the waste adjoyninge to theire severall tenements and enjoyed the profitts of the same. The value of which cottages wee have apporconed and sett in the value of the respective tenements of which they are taken to be a parte, and for that cause were not particulerly expressed in the survey of the said Mannor, but considering that the same may be prejudiciall to the purchaser wee desire that the said survey formerly retorned by us may be amended and the said cottages therein inserted as is before specified.'

[Sd] Hore Taylor Gentleman

INDEX OF PLACE NAMES

Where place-names have been firmly identified, the modern name is used in the index. In other cases the name as spelled in the text is used. When more than one spelling is used in the text for an unidentified place, all spellings are given. In the case of place-names such as Hendra and Pengelly which are found in more than one manor, they are distinguished by the name of the parish or manor in which they occur. Roman numerals refer to the Introduction in Part I.

Stony Island, 134
Stoute, 228
Stratton: parish, 8, 74, 163; Sanctuary, xvi, xx, xxi, 163–4
Sturts, in Climsland Prior, 34
Sutton: in Carnedon Prior, 25; Pool, xv, xxi, 241–2; Prior, 242; Valletorte, 196
Swimbridge, 222

TALA BROOK, 8
Talfrew Commons, 179
Talland parish, 63, 105, 106, 109
Talskidy, xv, xvi, xix, xxi, 165
Talvemeth, 47
Tamar river, x, 8, 13, 21–2, 80, 129, 151, 152, 161, 197; fishing in, 21
Tamerton, 7
Tamsquite, 187
Tavistock Abbey, 13
Tean: Island, 138; Sound, 138
Tehidy, 74
Teigncombe, 239
Teigne river, 240
Tedbridge, 226
Tedburn St Mary, 221
Tempello, 83
Termigo, 144
Tetcott, 218
Tewington, xv, xix, xxi, 1, 2, 53, 165–73, 206
Thankes Bay, 216
Thorn, 239, 240
Throwson, 240
Tibesta, xv, xix, xxi, 174–9
Timpethie, 180
Tintagel, xv, xix, xxi, 180–4; Castle, 180; parish, 55, 61, 181
Tinten, xv, xix, xxi, 185–90; Mill, 188
Tolcarne, 45; Higher, 115
Toller, 143
Toll's Island, 143
Torniscombe Wood, 12
Torpoint, 198
Torr, 157
Todesworthy, 14–5, 21
Towan, in St Agnes parish, 210
Towednack, 105
Towyn, 168, 172
Tramagenna, 59
Trayland, 87
Trebarra, 61
Trebartha, 30
Trebarwith, 184
Trebell, 116
Treburgie, 87
Trecaine, 176–7
Trecarne, 55
Trecarrell, 34
Treclugo, 54
Trecoliecke, 116
Trecombe, 160
Treculliacks, 193
Tredarrup, 39
Tredown, 198
Treefrees, Trefreies, Trefrize, 30, 34, 35, 125
Treforda, 55
Trefrew, 55, 57, 60 (*see* p. vi)
Tregamarras, 174

Tregamere, xv, xix, xxi, 190–1
Treganhatham, 190
Tregantallan, 193
Tregantle: in Gready, 42; in Trematon, 196, 197
Tregarick, Treggarick: in Killigarth, 65; in Tinten, 187, 188
Tregarthingrell, 144
Tregassicke, 46
Tregassow, 93
Tregate, 183
Tregath, 55
Tregatillian, 115, 120
Tregatta, 180
Tregenna: in St Ives, 105; in St Mawgan in Pydar, 115
Tregensith, 175
Tregenwin Down, 60
Tregerry, 39
Tregidgeo, 174
Tregiswin, 46
Tregoffe, 193
Tregoiffe, 33, 34
Tregols, 93
Tregondy, 212
Tregonissy, 204
Tregonjohn, 175
Tregooden, 188
Tregoodwell, 56
Tregoose, 44
Tregorianwartha, 93
Tregreenwell, 55, 59
Tregray, 39 (*see* p. vi)
Tregrie Lake, 39
Tregurra, 94
Tregwellin, 116
Trehane, 197
Trehenna, 196
Trehidland, 80
Trehill, 76
Trehingsta, 33
Trehinquethicke, 46
Trehurst, 64–5
Treisin, 174
Treknow, 182, 183
Trelabe, in Carnedon Prior, 26
Trelabe, Lower and Upper, in Climsland Prior, 33, 34
Treladrin, 191
Trelane, 154
Trelawgan, 115
Trelawne, 108
Trelay: in Killigarth, 65; in St Gennys, 208
Trelill, 44
Treliver, 115
Trelowarth, 46
Trelowia, xv, xix, xxi, 191–3
Trelubbas, 45
Trelugan, xv, xix, xxi, 193–5
Trelugon, 194
Tremabe, 83
Tremabyn, 42, 116
Trematon, xv, xvii, xix, xxi, 74, 126, 129, 195–202; Borough, 197, 198; Castle, 195
Tremayne, 191
Trembleth, 115
Trembraze, 85
Tremeer, 181
Tremenhere, 44

INDEX OF PERSONAL NAMES

INDEX OF SUBJECTS

Roman numerals (in lower case) refer to the pages of the Introduction; arabic numerals to the Text. The index is intended to show points of interest and is not exhaustive. Many words such as 'wood', 'waste', 'down', and 'moor' occur on almost every page and are not indexed.